Recovery Dharma

Recovery Dharma

*How to Use Buddhist
Practices and Principles
to Heal the Suffering
of Addiction*

version 1.0, August 2019

Recovery Dharma
www.recoverydharma.org

copyright © 2019 Recovery Dharma

ISBN: 978-1-08604-000-5

literature@recoverydharma.org

TABLE OF CONTENTS

PREFACE

Once we make a decision to recover from addiction—to substances, habits, people, whatever—it can be scary. The feeling is often one of loss and loneliness, because recovery can shake our sense of identity, our idea of who we are. *Who will I be if I let my addiction go?* Change can be hard to face, even if we know we're letting go of something that's a danger to us. For many of us, the first and most significant challenge was finding a safe and stable place to begin healing.

This is a book about using Buddhist practices and principles to recover from addiction, but you don't need to become a Buddhist to benefit from this program. One of the most revolutionary things the Buddha taught was that the mind is not only the source of great suffering—due to craving, greed, anger, and confusion—but the cure for that suffering as well. So what we're doing is using an ancient, proven way to literally change our minds. And we're choosing to trust in our own potential for wisdom and compassion for others *and* ourselves.

What you have in your hands is a collaboration from many members of our community. It's intended to be a friendly guide for those new to this path as well as long-term practitioners. It's structured around what are sometimes called the "three jewels of Buddhism:" **the Buddha** (the potential for our own awakening and the goal of the path), **the Dharma** (how we get there), and **the Sangha** (who we travel with). We'll share how we have used this program to recover from addiction and the ways we've made it our own: not as a one-size-fits-all approach, but as a dynamic set of tools and techniques that anyone can use to find relief from the suffering of addiction.

WHAT IS RECOVERY DHARMA?

The word *dharma* doesn't have a single English meaning. It's a word in an ancient language called Sanskrit, and it can be translated as "truth," "phenomena," or "the nature of things." When it's capitalized, the word *Dharma* usually means the teachings of the Buddha and the practices based on those teachings.

The Buddha knew that all human beings, to one degree or another, struggle with craving—the powerful, sometimes blinding desire to change our thoughts, feelings, and circumstances. Those of us who experience addiction have been more driven to use substances or behaviors to do this, but the underlying craving is the same. And even though the Buddha didn't talk specifically about addiction, he understood the obsessive nature of the human mind. He understood our attachment to pleasure and aversion to pain. He understood the extreme lengths we can sometimes go to, chasing what we want to feel and running away from the feelings we fear. And he found a solution.

This book describes a way to free ourselves from the suffering of addiction using Buddhist practices and principles. This program leads to recovery from addiction to substances like alcohol and drugs, and also from what we refer to as *process addictions*. We can also become addicted to sex, gambling, technology, work, codependence, shopping, food, media, self-harm, lying, stealing, obsessive worrying. This is a path to freedom from any repetitive and habitual behavior that causes suffering.

Many of us who have found our way here might be new to Buddhism. There are unfamiliar words, concepts, and ways of looking at the world. It can be intimidating and uncomfortable to sit in a meeting with people throwing around words like karma, Dharma, Sangha, and Buddha. If you have felt this way, you're not alone. The purpose of this book is to lay out our path and practice in a clear and simple way that can be of use to people who are brand new to recovery and to Buddhism, as well as those with some experience. It describes the original Buddhist teachings to show where our program comes from. It introduces the essence of Buddhism's basic teachings—the Four Noble Truths—in a way that shows how practicing the Eightfold Path is a pragmatic tool-kit for dealing with the challenges of both early and long-term recovery.

This is a renunciation-based program. Regardless of the type of addiction we identify with, all of our members commit to a basic abstinence from the substance or behavior of our addiction. For those of us whose addictions involve things like food and technology from which complete abstinence may not be possible, renunciation will mean something different, based on thoughtful boundaries and intentions in our behaviors. For some of us, abstinence from things like obsessive sexual behavior or compulsively seeking out love and relationships may be necessary as we work to understand and find meaningful boundaries. Many of us have found that after renouncing our primary addiction for a period of time, other harmful behaviors and process addictions become apparent in our lives. But rather than getting discouraged, we found that we can also meet these behaviors with compassion and patient investigation. We believe recovery is a lifelong, holistic process of peeling back layers of habits and conditioned behaviors to find our own, sometimes hidden, potential for awakening.

Our program is peer-led: we don't follow any one teacher or leader. We support each other as partners walking the path of recovery together. This is not a program based in dogma or religion, but in finding the truth for ourselves. This is wisdom that has worked for us, but it is not the only path. It's fully compatible with other spiritual paths and programs of recovery. We know from our own experience that true recovery is only possible with the intention of radical honesty, understanding, awareness, and integrity, and we trust you to discover your own path. We believe this program can help you do just that.

Ours is a program that asks us to never stop growing. It asks us to own our choices and be responsible for our own healing. It's based on kindness, generosity, forgiveness, and deep compassion. We do not rely on tools of shame and fear as motivation. We know these haven't worked in our own individual pasts, and have often created more struggle and suffering through relapse and discouragement. The courage it takes to recover from addiction is ultimately courage of the heart, and we aim to support each other as we commit to this brave work.

Many of us have spent our lives beating ourselves up. In this program, we renounce violence and doing harm, including the harm and violence we do to ourselves. We believe in the healing power of forgiveness. We put our trust in our own potential to awaken and recover, in the Four Noble Truths of the Buddha, and in the people we meet and connect with in meetings and throughout our journey in recovery.

The truth is that we can never truly escape the circumstances and conditions that are part of the human condition. We've tried that already—through drugs and alcohol, through sex and codependency, through gambling and technology, through work and shopping, through food or the restriction of food, through obsession and the futile attempts to control our experiences and feelings—and we're here because we realized it didn't work. This is a program that asks us to recognize and accept that some pain and disappointment will always be present, to investigate the unskillful ways we have dealt with that pain in the past, and to develop a habit of understanding, compassion, and mercy toward our own pain, the pain of others, and the pain we have caused others due to our ignorance and confusion. That acceptance is what brings freedom from the suffering that made our pain unbearable.

This book is only an introduction to a path that can bring liberation and freedom from the cycle of suffering created by addiction. The intention, and the hope, is that every person on the path will be empowered to make it their own.

May you be happy.

May you be at ease.

May you be free from suffering.

Where to Begin

So how *can* we use Buddhism for our recovery? There are three ways in which we focus our energy: not step-by-step, but in a holistic way as our insight and our awareness grow.

We come to understand the Four Noble Truths and use them as a guide for our own path of recovery. This program doesn't ask us to believe in anything other than our own potential to wake up: just allowing ourselves to believe that it's possible, or even that it *might* be possible. We begin to believe that our own efforts will make a difference. This is the realization that there is a way to recover and then the decision to start that process.

As we learn about the Four Noble Truths—including the Eightfold Path that leads to the end of the suffering caused by addiction—we put these principles into practice in our lives. This book includes an introduction to these truths, and there are many ways to continue studying them. The Eightfold Path is a guide to a non-harming way of being in the world. It's not just a philosophy, but a plan of action.

Meditation is an essential part of the program. This book has some basic instructions so you can start right away. Most of us have found it very helpful to attend meetings that include an opportunity to practice meditation with others. A key to this program is establishing a regular meditation practice, in and outside of meetings. This will help us begin the process of investigating our own minds, our reactivity, and our behavior. We look deeply at the nature and causes of our suffering so we can find a path to freedom that's based on authentic self-knowledge.

The following chapters talk about these three aspects of the program—the "three jewels" of Buddha, Dharma, and Sangha—as a way of developing the wisdom, ethical conduct, and spiritual practice that we have found leads to recovery. We hope that people and groups will use this book in ways that are useful for their own processes of recovery. We offer some suggestions in that spirit. You're invited to take what works for you and leave the rest.

At the end of each section are a series of questions to explore. These Inquiries can be used as part of a formal process of self-investigation with a mentor, wise friend, or group; as tools to explore a specific life situation; as guides for a daily self-inquiry practice; or as meeting discussion topics. A wise friend or mentor can be of great help in deepening your understanding, and we encourage you to reach out to people you encounter at meetings. Supportive friendships are an integral part of the practice. The questions may bring up shame, guilt, or sadness; or, for some, they may potentially activate trauma. It can be very beneficial to get supports set up ahead of time, such as taking the questions only one at a time, timing the work so you can have a chance to engage in self-care afterwards, and so forth. The intent of the questions is to deepen our practice so we can experience relief sooner, not to bring us more suffering.

Our path is not a checklist, but is rather a practice in which we choose where and how to invest our energy in a way that is both wise and compassionate toward ourselves and others. We do not "complete" our journey based on how much we meditate or how many meetings we go to or how many written inventories we've completed. The practice of the Eightfold Path helps us develop insight and self-compassion as we begin to look into the causes and conditions that led to our own suffering with addiction. The tools will come to bear the signs of wear and markings of our using them.

This path doesn't have an end. Your life, like all of ours, will probably continue to present you with challenges. What the path *does* offer, however, is a way out of the suffering that our habitual reactions to challenges often bring, and an end to the illusion of escape we tried to find in substances or behaviors. It's a way to break our own chains with our own hands. It's a path of freedom.

THE PRACTICE

Renunciation: We understand *addiction* to describe the overwhelming craving and compulsive use of substances or behaviors in order to escape present-time reality, either by clinging to pleasure or running from pain. We commit to the intention of abstinence from alcohol and other addictive substances. For those of us recovering from process addictions, particularly those for which complete abstinence is not possible, we also identify and commit to wise boundaries around our harmful behaviors, preferably with the help of a mentor or therapeutic professional.

Meditation: We commit to the intention of developing a daily meditation practice. We use meditation as a tool to investigate our actions, intentions, and reactivity. Meditation is a personal practice, and we commit to finding a balanced effort toward this and other healthy practices that are appropriate to our own journey on the path.

Meetings: We attend recovery meetings whenever possible, in person and/or online. Some may wish to be part of other recovery fellowships and Buddhist communities. In early recovery, it is recommended to attend a recovery meeting as often as possible. For many that may mean every day. We also commit to becoming an active part of the community, offering our own experiences and service wherever possible.

The Path: We commit to deepening our understanding of the Four Noble Truths and to practicing the Eightfold Path in our daily lives.

Inquiry and Investigation: We explore the Four Noble Truths as they relate to our addictive behavior through writing and sharing in-depth, detailed Inquiries. These can be worked with the guidance of a mentor, in partnership with a trusted friend, or with a group. As we complete our written Inquiries, we undertake to hold ourselves accountable and take direct responsibility for our actions, which includes making amends for the harm we have caused in our past. .

Sangha, Wise Friends, Mentors: We cultivate relationships within a recovery community, to both support our own recovery and support the recovery of others. After we have completed significant work on our Inquiries, established a meditation practice, and achieved renunciation from our addictive behaviors, we can then become mentors to help others on their path to liberation from addiction. Anyone with any period of time of renunciation and practice can be of service to others in their sangha. When mentors are not available, a group of wise friends can act as partners in self-inquiry and support each other's practice.

Growth: We continue our study of these Buddhist practices through reading, listening to dharma talks, visiting and becoming members of recovery and spiritual sanghas, and attending meditation or dharma retreats when we believe these practices will contribute to our understanding and wisdom. We undertake a lifelong journey of growth and awakening.

Awakening: *Buddha*

Most of us enter into recovery with one goal in mind: to stop the suffering that got us here in the first place, whether that was drinking, using drugs, stealing, eating, gambling, sex, codependency, technology, or other process addictions. As newcomers, most of us would be satisfied with simple damage control. We want to stop harming ourselves or others in particular ways.

You're reading this right now because you had enough wisdom to start seeking the end of the suffering of your addiction. You've already taken the first step on the path to your own awakening. Everyone who has made the wise intention to recover, wherever they are on their path, has accessed that pure, wise part of themselves that the wreckage of addiction can never touch.

So many of us have hearts that are tender and worn raw from the suffering we've experienced. Many of us have collected layers of trauma which often led us to seek temporary relief in our addictive behavior. But then, through our addiction, we added more layers of demoralization and shame that hardened around our hearts. On top of those layers are the ones we built for our protection: all the ways we've run from pain, all the ways we've pushed people away in fear of being vulnerable, all the ways we've shut parts of ourselves off in order to adapt to what often feels like a hostile world.

We started to recover when we let ourselves believe in the part of us that's still there beneath all those layers we've collected and built—the pure, radiant, courageous heart where we find our potential for awakening. Who were we before the world got to us? Who are we beyond the obsession of our conditioned minds? Who are we beneath all our walls and heartbreak? Despite the

1

trauma, addiction, fear, and shame, there is a still and centered part of us that remains whole. There is a part of us that's not traumatized, that's not addicted, that's not ruled by fear or shame. This is where wisdom comes from, and it's the foundation of our recovery.

If you're at the beginning of your recovery journey, it may seem impossible to access this part of you. But the reason you're here is because you already did. It's because you felt some small glimmer of hope—maybe born out of desperation—that there might be a way out, that things could change if you took wise action and reached out for help. Maybe it feels impossible to have faith in this part of you, to believe that you have the potential to be someone capable of wisdom and kindness and ethical deeds, to believe you can be the source of your own healing and awakening. But don't worry. Recovery doesn't happen all at once. The path is a lifetime of individual steps. It's not only the Buddha's example that shows us the way, it's also the examples of people in our recovery communities who have gone through what we have and made it through to the other side. They show us we can, too.

So what does the Buddha have to do with recovery?

There are two ways in which we use the word **Buddha,** which means "awakened." First, it is the title given to a person named Siddhartha Gautama, a man who lived in modern-day Nepal and India roughly 2,500 years ago. After many years of meditation and ethical practice, he discovered a path that leads to liberation or awakening and the end of suffering, and that's why Siddhartha came to be known as the Buddha.

The second usage of the word Buddha follows from the first. Buddha can refer not only to the historical figure but also to the idea of awakening: the fact that each of us has within ourselves the potential to awaken to the same understanding as the original Buddha. When we take refuge in the Buddha, we take refuge not in Siddhartha as a man, but in the fact that he was able to find freedom from his suffering. He was human just like us, and experienced suffering just like us. He found liberation from it, and so can we.

The Story of the Original Buddha

To understand the nature of this awakening and what it is we're aiming at, it helps to know something about the life of the man named Siddhartha Gautama.

There are many versions of the traditional story of the Buddha. Some of them are very mythical, while some of them are more down to earth. It's been said that Siddhartha was a prince, that he was wealthy, and that he was born into privilege, sheltered from much of the suffering of the world. The story goes that young Siddhartha sneaked away from his palace and saw people suffering from old age, sickness, and death. He realized that no amount of privilege could protect him from this suffering. Wealth wouldn't prevent it. Comfort wouldn't prevent it. Pleasure wouldn't prevent it. Despite having a life of ease, Siddhartha still found that he experienced suffering and dissatisfaction. He was born with everything, but it wasn't enough.

This persistent dissatisfaction with life, whether dramatic or subtle, was referred to as **dukkha** in the language of the Buddha's time, a word we still use today. All humans experience dukkha, but some of us—particularly those of us who have struggled with addiction—seem to experience it on a more intense level, and with worse consequences. What is addiction but the consistent and nagging feeling of "not enough?" What is addiction other than being constantly unsatisfied?

3

Siddhartha saw clearly that pain was an unavoidable part of life, and he became determined to find a way to put an end to it. He left his family and tried, for a while, the life of an ascetic—the most extreme opposite to his previous life of comfort and wealth. As an ascetic, he sat in extremely uncomfortable postures meditating for long periods of time. He slept very little. He ate very little. He even tried breathing very little. He thought that, since material comfort hadn't brought about an end to suffering, maybe the opposite of material comfort would. But it didn't. Pushed to the brink of death, Siddhartha abandoned the idea of extreme asceticism and instead chose what he came to call "the middle path."

Siddhartha realized that both the extremes of pleasure and denial of pleasure had gotten him nowhere nearer to liberation. Neither extreme had given relief from his suffering. So he set off on his own to meditate. Sitting beneath a Bodhi tree, he meditated deeply and discovered the path that leads to the end of suffering. He looked within himself for his own liberation, and he found it.

What Siddhartha found meditating under the Bodhi tree is what we refer to as the **Dharma**, or the "Truth." It's what the path of Buddhism is based on. Central to this path are the Four Noble Truths and the Eightfold Path, which will be explained in the next chapter.

Siddhartha was called the Buddha, or "The One Who Woke Up," because the way most people go through life was thought to be like dreaming or being in a trance. The Buddha spent the rest of his life developing the Dharma into a simple but sophisticated system. He shared it with anyone who would listen, dedicating himself to a life of service to free everybody from suffering. He bucked the trends of his time by letting women and the poorest class of citizens become monastics. Everybody was welcome in his *Sangha*, his spiritual community. Central to his teachings was that liberation is available to all—to the most broken and oppressed among us, to the sick, to the powerless, to those who have lost everything, to those who have nothing left to lose. All of us, even the most addicted, the most lost, can find our way to awakening.

Walking in the Footsteps of the Buddha

The story of the Buddha may seem far removed from our everyday reality, but his life, both before and after his awakening, offers us a model for our own lives. Probably all of us can relate to the suffering that seems to be unavoidable in life. In some way or another, the signs of aging, sickness, or death have touched us all. We've experienced the truth of impermanence—the highs and pleasures we achieved in our addictions always eventually wore off, but we kept chasing them anyway. We've endured other forms of suffering, some of it self-inflicted and some at the hands of others. And we've dealt with the subtle forms of dukkha: the annoyances with others, the boredom, the loss of what we want, the inability to keep what we have, the impatience with life, the refusal to accept what is. And what have we done with these experiences of suffering? Maybe we tried to change them. Maybe we tried to avoid them. Maybe we tried to find something more pleasurable to replace what was unpleasant.

It's at this point that most of our stories start to look different than Siddhartha's, and it's this difference that led us to this program. Instead of deeply understanding suffering, we found ways to avoid it or replace it with something we found more pleasurable. For some of us, that came in the form of drinking or using. For others, it came in the form of sex, relationships, food, self-harming, technology addiction, workaholism, or gambling. And for a lot of us, our stories contain some version of "all of the above." Whatever our behavior was, we found that it was just a temporary solution that always led to deeper suffering for ourselves and others.

We've come to realize that our stories don't have to continue like this. The life of Siddhartha, and the lives of the countless people we meet in recovery who have found an end to the suffering of addiction, prove to us that there is another way.

We, too, can look back upon our own lives and see clearly the path that brought us here. We can examine our own actions and intentions and come to understand how we shape our own future. And we can gain insight into the nature of our own suffering and follow a path that leads to less harm and less suffering.

This is a path of practice. While the Buddha can be an ideal that inspires us, he won't do the work for us. The Buddha wasn't a God. There's nothing miraculous about the path we follow. We believe, and experience has shown us, that good results come when we put the necessary effort into our own recovery. This is a program of empowerment: we take responsibility for our own actions and intentions. The Sangha is here to help us along the way.

None of us is expected to become an ascetic. We don't have to become monks or nuns, and we don't have to meditate for hours each day. We don't have to become Buddhists. But we have found that the path outlined in the Four Noble Truths can lead us to liberation from both the suffering of addiction and the suffering that comes from simply being human, and we trust in the potential in all of us to find freedom from this suffering.

The Truth: *Dharma*

As people who have struggled with addiction, we're already intimately familiar with the truth of suffering. Even if we've never heard of the Buddha, at some level we already understand the core of his teachings: that in this life, there is suffering.

It can be incredibly liberating to hear this said so plainly and directly. No one is trying to convince or convert us. No one is telling us we have to believe something. No one is sugarcoating our experience. For once, it feels like we're being told the truth.

The Buddha also taught the way to free ourselves from this suffering. The heart of these teachings (which we call the Dharma) is the Four Noble Truths. These truths, and the corresponding commitments, are the foundation of our program:

1. There is suffering. We commit to understanding the truth of suffering.
2. There is a cause of suffering. We commit to understanding that craving leads to suffering.
3. There is an end to suffering. We commit to understanding and experiencing that less craving leads to less suffering.
4. There is a path that leads to the end of suffering. We commit to cultivating the path.

Like a map that shows us the path, these truths help us find our way in recovery.

The First Noble Truth:
There is Suffering

Some of the ways in which we suffer are obvious, like hunger, pain, disappointment, and feeling separated or excluded. Some are less obvious, like feelings of anxiety, stress, and uncertainty. We suffer as we struggle with aging, sickness, and death. As much as we want to hold onto the things, people, and feelings we like, we'll always have to deal with separation and loss. There's suffering any time we want things to be different than they are.

The First Noble Truth rests on the understanding that our lives are unsatisfactory due to the fact that experiences are impermanent and impersonal. Our senses (which the Buddha understood to include not just hearing, seeing, smelling, tasting, and touch, but also thinking) are unreliable and temporary, which means that the way we experience and make sense of the world is constantly changing. We suffer because we keep expecting these temporary experiences to satisfy our craving for pleasure or to avoid pain.

Many of us have suffered by trying, and failing, to control our dependencies, habits, and addictions. We've used every kind of willpower, bargaining, planning, and magical thinking, each time imagining the result would be different, and beating ourselves up when it turned out the same.

How many times did we promise: "Just this one last time, then I'm done? I'll just use or drink on the weekends, or only after work, or only on special occasions. I'll never drink in the morning. I won't do the hard stuff. I'll never get high alone. I'll never use at work or around my family. I'll never drink and drive. I'll never use needles."

How many diets have we tried? How many times have we said we wouldn't binge, or purge, or restrict calories, or over-exercise?

How many times have we looked at the scars on our arms and vowed to never cut again? How many times have we let our wounds heal, only to break them open once more?

How many limits have we set on ourselves around technology or work, only to get sucked back in? How many times have we vowed to have no more one-night stands, vowed to stay away from certain people or places or websites? How many times have we crossed our own boundaries and been consumed by shame?

How many mornings did we wake up hating ourselves, vowing to never do again what we did last night, only to find ourselves repeating the same mistake again just a few hours later?

How many times did we attempt to cure our addictions with therapy, with self-help books, with cleanses, with more exercise, by changing a job or relationship? How many times did we move, thinking our shadow wouldn't follow us?

How many promises did we make? How many times did we break those promises?

Having suffered and struggled with addiction in its many forms, we've come to understand this first truth as it relates to recovery: Addiction is suffering. We suffer when we obsess, when we cling and grasp onto all of the delusions of addiction, all the impermanent solutions to our discomfort and pain. We've tried to cure our suffering by using the very substances and behaviors that create more discomfort and pain. In all of our attempts to control our habits, we've still been clinging to the illusion that we can somehow control our experiences of the world. We're still caught in the prison of suffering.

In fact, we're reinforcing the walls of that prison, building them taller and stronger as we act on our addictions.

Liberation comes when we gain a clear understanding of where our real power lies, and where we are throwing it away.

This is a program of empowerment. It's a path of letting go of behavior that no longer serves us and cultivating that which does.

Trauma and Attachment Injury

For many of us, suffering also exists as trauma. Trauma is often described as the psychological damage that occurs after living through an extremely frightening or distressing event or situation. It's caused by an overwhelming amount of stress that exceeds our ability to cope, and may make it hard to function even long after the event. Trauma can come from childhood experiences or from events that occur in our adulthood. It can be sudden, or it can develop over time from a series of events that changed how we perceived the world. While trauma frequently comes from life-threatening events, any situation that leaves one feeling emotionally or physically in danger can be traumatic.

It's important to note that it's not the objective facts of the event alone that determine how traumatic it is, it's the subjective emotional perception of the person who experiences it. Generally, the more terror and helplessness we feel, and the longer that terror lasts, the more likely it is that we'll be traumatized.

Attachment injury can be just as insidious and harmful as trauma, and can have the same impact. It's defined as an emotional wound to a core relationship with a caregiver, often caused by abuse, neglect, or inconsistency of care in early childhood. Attachment injury and trauma can impact our recovery and meditation practice in slightly different ways. With trauma we may feel fear (even panic) or distrust when asked to "sit" in meditation, even when intellectually we know we're in a safe place with a supportive group. It may be triggering to be asked to be present in our bodies and minds, or to focus on our breath. Attachment injury may show up as a hesitation to trust people or a process, as a reluctance to be part of a recovery group or sangha, or as a core belief that we don't belong. In this case, the nurturing thing to do for ourselves might be to lean into this discomfort and compassionately engage and investigate the stories we're telling ourselves about not belonging. Again, it's key to become aware of the nature of the harm we carry with us. Trauma and attachment injury may require different ways of feeling safe and supported. You should always do whatever is most compassionate for yourself in the moment, and seek outside help when you need it.

Trauma and attachment issues are relevant to suffering and addiction because the impact can be intense. Studies show that a majority of people who struggle with addiction have experienced trauma at some point in their lives. The same system that serves to keep us safe from harm is also the one that fuels the mechanisms of aversion and craving that perpetuate suffering. This system can be overactive when trauma is present because it perceives a very real threat, and the body often responds with feelings of helplessness, fear, and vulnerability. This system can be easily thrown into overdrive when one's life experience screams: "You're not safe! Danger! Danger!"

For some people, symptoms of trauma may be increasingly severe and last long after the events that originally caused the trauma have ended. Many of us have intrusive thoughts that seem to come out of the

11

blue, or we feel confusion or mood swings we can't tie to specific events. Traumatic responses may lead us to avoid activities or places that trigger memories of the event. We can become socially isolated and withdrawn, and lose interest in things we used to enjoy. Trauma may mean we're easily startled, edgy, or dysfunctional during sex or other activities, or unusually alert to potential danger. Overwhelming fear, anxiety, detachment and isolation, shame, and anger may become background states of our activities. There are many other effects of trauma that may be triggered by social interactions or even during work or meditation—areas that may seem disconnected from the original events.

Trauma and attachment issues can certainly lead to the fear, anger, anxiety, and loneliness that are common responses to the experience of life. But, at a deeper level, trauma makes it harder for us to cope in general, to form healthy or safe relationships, to develop an identity in the world, or to defend ourselves. No two of us will react to the same experience in the same way, but this truth points to the fact that certain kinds of experience in our pasts can affect our responses later in life. This is key to understanding dukkha, and to meeting our experience with compassion and kindness rather than judgment (not only for others but also for ourselves), which is an essential part of recovery.

Many of us turned to addictive substances and behaviors as a way to cope with our trauma. In some ways, running from the pain of our experiences through our addictions was itself a survival technique when it felt like we wouldn't be able to live through the pain of our memories. While this may have provided some temporary relief, it did nothing to actually heal the pain of our trauma, and often led to even more pain.

Our trauma is not our fault, but healing from it is our responsibility, and our right. Developing understanding and compassion toward the way trauma affects our reactions to events or circumstances *now* is an important part of that healing.

Questions for Inquiry of the First Noble Truth:

Begin by making a list of the behaviors and actions associated with your addiction(s) that you consider harmful. Without exaggerating or minimizing, think about the things you have done that have caused harm to yourself and others.

For each behavior listed, write how you have suffered because of that behavior, and write how others have suffered because of that behavior. List any other costs or negative consequences you can think of, such as finances, health, relationships, sexual relations, or missed opportunities.

Do you notice any patterns? What are they? What are the ways that you might avoid or reduce suffering for yourself and others if you change these patterns?

How have your addictive behaviors been a response to trauma and pain? What are some ways you can respond to trauma and pain that nurture healing rather than avoiding?

The Second Noble Truth:
The Cause of Suffering

As people who have become dependent on substances and behaviors, we've all experienced the sense of failure and hopelessness that comes from trying, and failing, to let go of our fixations. Addiction itself increases our suffering by creating a hope that both pleasure and escape can be permanent. We go through this suffering again and again because substances or behaviors can only give us temporary relief to our pain, our unhappiness, and our lost or damaged sense of self.

Our refusal to accept the way things are leads to wanting, or craving, which is the cause of suffering. We don't suffer because of the way things are, but because we want—or think we "need"—those things to be different. We suffer because we cling to the idea that we can satisfy our own cravings, while ignoring the conditions of the world around us. Above all, we cling to the idea that we can hold on to impermanent and unreliable things, things that can't ever lead to real satisfaction or lasting happiness, without experiencing the suffering of one day losing them.

Clinging to impermanent solutions for suffering results in craving. We experience craving like a thirst, an unsatisfied longing, and it can become a driving force in our lives. If craving goes beyond simple desire, which is a natural part of life, it often leads us to fixation, obsession, and the delusional belief that we can't be happy without getting what we crave. It warps our intentions so that we make choices that harm ourselves and others. This repetitive craving and obsessive drive to satisfy it leads to what we now know as addiction. Addiction occupies the part of our mind that chooses—our will—and replaces compassion, kindness, generosity, honesty, and other intentions that might have been there. Many of us experience addiction as the loss of our freedom to choose; it's the addiction that seems to be making our choices for us.

In the way we "must have" food, shelter, or water, our mind can tell us we "must have" some substance, buy or steal something, satisfy some lust, keep acting until we achieve some "needed" result; that we must protect ourselves at all cost and attack people with whom we disagree, or people who have something we want. This "need" also leads to an unsettled or agitated state of mind that tells us we'll only be happy if we get certain results or feel a certain way. We want to be someone we're not, or we don't want to be who we are.

Conditions or circumstances in and of themselves don't cause suffering. They can cause pain or unpleasant experiences, but we add suffering on top of this when we think we "need" those circumstances to be different. We create even more suffering when we act out in ways that deny the reality of the circumstances and the reality of impermanence. Craving is the underlying motive that fuels unwise actions that create suffering.

Questions for Inquiry of the Second Noble Truth:
List situations, circumstances, and feelings that you may have used harmful behavior to try and avoid.

List the emotions, sensations, and thoughts that come to mind when you abstain. Are there troubling memories, shame, grief, or unmet needs hiding behind the craving? How can you meet these with compassion and patience?

What things did you give up in your desire to cling to impermanent and unreliable solutions? For example, did you give up relationships, financial security, health, opportunities, legal standing, or other important things to maintain your addictive behaviors? What made the addiction more important to you than any of these things you gave up?

Are there any beliefs you cling to that fuel craving and aversion, beliefs that deny the truth of impermanence, or beliefs about how things in life "should" be? What are they?

The Third Noble Truth:
The End of Suffering

It is possible to end our suffering. When we come to understand the nature of our craving and realize that all our experiences are temporary by nature, we can begin a more skillful way to live with the dissatisfaction that is part of being human. We don't need to be torn apart by our thoughts and feelings that say, "I have to have more of that," or "I'll do anything to get rid of that." The Third Noble Truth is that the end of craving is possible. Each of us has the capacity for recovery.

We are responsible for our own actions and for the energy we give our thoughts and feelings. This means we have control over our own suffering, because the unpleasant emotions take place within us: we create them through our response to experience. We don't need to depend on anyone or anything else to remove the causes of our suffering. We may not be able to control anything "out there," but we *can* learn to choose what we think, say, and do. We come to understand that if our thoughts, words, and actions are driven by greed, hatred, or confusion, we are creating suffering. And so, if we let go of these actions, we can avoid suffering in the future. We can choose to give up the causes of disturbing and unpleasant emotions, knowing that virtuous actions result in happiness and un-virtuous actions result in suffering. This is the true empowerment and freedom of recovery—recognizing that happiness and suffering are entirely up to us, based on how we choose to respond to our experiences.

Questions for Inquiry of the Third Noble Truth:
What makes it so hard to quit?

What resources are available to help you abstain and recover?

List reasons to believe you can recover. Also list your doubts. What might the wise and compassionate part of you—your Buddha nature—say about these doubts?

Practice "letting go" of something small. Notice that the craving doesn't last and that there's a little sense of relief when you let it pass. That's a little taste of freedom.

The Fourth Noble Truth:
The Path

The Buddha taught that by living ethically, practicing meditation, and developing wisdom and compassion, we can end the suffering we create by resisting, running from, and misunderstanding reality.

The Fourth Noble Truth is a summary of the essential elements to recovery, or awakening, called the Eightfold Path. The Path is a set of instructions, a practice, and a way to investigate and be aware of the conditioned responses we cling to. These are the eight factors of the Path:

- Wise Understanding
- Wise Intention
- Wise Speech
- Wise Action
- Wise Livelihood
- Wise Effort
- Wise Mindfulness
- Wise Concentration

These eight factors can be broken down into three groups: The Wisdom group of Wise Understanding and Intention; the Ethics group of Wise Speech, Action, and Livelihood; and the Concentration group of Wise Effort, Mindfulness, and Concentration.

Each of us will understand and practice each aspect of this Eightfold Path in our own way. We develop our wisdom, ethical practice, and concentration as far as we can in any given moment. As we come to a deeper understanding of the Four Noble Truths, we're able to bring more effort and concentration to letting go of our greed, hatred, and confusion. Our ethical development will cause us to reflect more deeply on the sources of our unwise actions.

The Eightfold Path is a way of life that each of us follows and practices to the best of our current understanding and capacity. The Path is not a religious journey, and has nothing to do with belief, prayer, worship, or ceremony. It's a guide to practice and a road that leads to a deep experience of the Noble Truths.

Questions for Inquiry of the Fourth Noble Truth:

Understanding that recovery and the ending of suffering is possible, what is your path to recovery and ending the suffering of addiction? Be honest about the challenges you might face, and the tools and resources you will use to meet those challenges.

What behavior can you change to more fully support your recovery?

What does it mean to you to take refuge in the Buddha, the Dharma, and the Sangha for your recovery?

The Eightfold Path

We've found that it's useful to make inquiry and investigation a normal part of our everyday routine, especially when we're feeling uncomfortable emotions or facing tough decisions. We can take a moment to pause and sit with whatever it is we're experiencing, identify our situation, and just allow it to be there, with compassion and without judgment, and then use the Eightfold Path as a guide to go inward and forward. In any situation, we can ask ourselves: "How can I apply the Eightfold Path?" It can also be beneficial to use the different parts of the Eightfold Path as an end-of-day reflection.

Wise Understanding

As people engaged in the world, rather than withdrawn from it, we can use Wise Understanding to live without clinging, attachment, or craving. By paying attention to our actions and the results of those actions, we can begin to change where our choices are leading. If we intend to act in ways that have positive results, and if we're aware of the true intention and the nature of our actions, then we'll see better results—*better* meaning less suffering and less harm.

The word *karma* literally means "action" or "doing." Any kind of intentional act—mental, verbal, or physical—is a kind of karma. Skillful or wise actions strengthen our sense of balance, kindness, compassion, loving, and equanimity. When we act unskillfully or unwisely—when we steal, lie, take advantage of somebody else, or cause intentional harm based on our own craving or delusions—it creates an immediate sense of imbalance. It fights with our intention to avoid harming others. Karma is determined by our intention

21

and applies to any volitional—purposeful—action. The result of our volitional actions may be an increase in our happiness or may lead to additional suffering. There is no actor apart from action, and there is no action without intention.

Unskillful actions leave us less able to meet the next challenge or pain we are faced with. For example, when we steal, we have to immediately justify to ourselves why our greed was more important than the harm we caused by taking. We must create a cover story, hide our actions, and adjust to the fear of getting caught. Ultimately, if the theft gets discovered, we might have to deal with financial or legal consequences, or face a lack of trust from our community. Similarly, when we're dishonest, we immediately focus energy on maintaining the untruth. We must emotionally carry the potential pain that is caused to others, and ourselves, if the lie is revealed.

This understanding of karma rests on the insight that we are responsible for our own happiness and misery, and that there is a cause to every experience of happiness or misery. From a Buddhist point of view, our choices— which are dependent on our present mental, moral, intellectual, and emotional conditions—decide the effects of our actions. If we act skillfully, with understanding and compassion, it's possible to cause positive, beneficial effects for ourselves and others. If we act with unskillful intention, we cause our own suffering.

This doesn't mean that we always have control over our experiences. No matter how skillfully we act, the external world—people, places, and things—might not give us what we want. This does not mean we have "bad karma," or that we've failed. It just means that we're not in control of everything and everyone. The point is that, regardless of what the outside world throws at us, we're responsible for how we respond to it and how we tend to our internal world. At the end of the day, we have the choice whether we go to bed as somebody who acted wisely and compassionately, or as somebody who didn't.

It's important to note that being responsible for our own happiness and suffering doesn't mean we're responsible for hurts or traumas that have been done to us by others, or by circumstances out of our control. Many of us have very real experiences of victimization, oppression, and trauma through no fault of our own. The pain from these experiences should be met with compassion and care, not minimized or pushed away. In recovery, we learn that we don't have to add an extra layer of suffering to this pain. We can begin to heal, rather than let these experiences control and limit us. Without discounting or ignoring the ongoing effects of trauma in our lives, we begin to understand that our reactions when that trauma comes up for us now can change our experience of suffering and happiness.

The Buddhist perspective is that our present mental, moral, intellectual, and emotional circumstances are the direct result of our actions and habits, both past and present. How we choose to respond when confronted with pain or discomfort will change our ability to skillfully deal with suffering when it arises. We can also take solace in the fact that we're not alone, that every person has difficult and unpleasant experiences. It's how we *respond* to pain that determines our experience.

Questions for Inquiry of Wise Understanding:
Think of a situation in your life that is causing confusion or unease.

- What is the truth of this situation?
- Are you seeing clearly, or are you getting lost in judgment, taking things personally in stories

you're telling yourself, or repeating past messages you've internalized? How?

- Is your vision clouded by greed, hatred, confusion, clinging, attachment, or craving? How?

In what situations and parts of your life do you have the most difficulty separating desire from need? Are there areas or relationships where the drive to get what you desire overshadows any other consideration? Has this changed as you began or continue in recovery?

Are there parts of your life where you are driven to continue unpleasant experiences because you think you "must" or "need to?"

How is karma—the law of cause and effect—showing up right now? Where in your life are you dealing with the effects or aftermath of action you took in the past, both positive and negative?

Wise Intention

Wise Intention describes the attitude or approach we take toward ourselves and the world. We can choose non-harming by avoiding actions that have harmful results, detaching from the cravings that seem overwhelming in the moment, and developing a kind and compassionate stance toward both ourselves and the world. Wise Intention leads us to stop doing things based on ill-will, hatred, violence, and selfishness. It impacts all our relationships: with ourselves, other people, our community, and the world as a whole.

Wise Intention is deciding to act in ways that produce good karma and to avoid actions that produce bad karma. We start by looking at the kinds of thoughts that cause us to act in wholesome or unwholesome ways. If our thoughts are based on confusion, fear, and greed, then our actions will bring bad results. If our thoughts are based on generosity, compassion, and avoiding clinging, then our actions will bring good results. Thoughts that are based in lovingkindness and goodwill, that are free from the desire or intention to cause harm, lead us to act in a wholesome manner.

There may be times when we don't necessarily *want* to act in a wholesome manner. We may know what's the right thing to do, but just don't want to do it. It's in these moments when we can focus on our intention. Maybe we aren't ready to do the difficult thing, to quit a certain behavior, to set a boundary, or forgive someone for whom we hold a resentment. But we can set the *intention* to do so, and investigate our willingness in meditation by repeating statements like "May I have the willingness to forgive.... May I have the willingness to quit smoking (or skip that piece of cake, or stay off the internet tonight, etc.).... May I have the willingness to make amends to my partner."

The first choice we can make in Wise Intention is that of **generosity**. Generosity teaches us how to let go of our self-centeredness, to let go of clinging to ideas of "mine" and "me." Selfishness, or self-centeredness, is one of the ways we justify and cling to our addictive behaviors. Generosity comes from the awareness that we're holding on too tightly to our selfishness in a given moment. The karmic result of looking at the world only through the lens of "me" and "mine" and "what I want" leads to loneliness, separation, and dissatisfaction. Letting go of this clinging can be the solution.

Without generosity, the mind is confined to a small, tight space. Anything that's not about "me and mine" is off limits. During times in our lives when we become dependent, our world becomes focused on satisfying our cravings, on holding onto what we want right now. We get sucked into the reactivity of survival mode, believing that we must have our addictive substance or behavior to survive. Our "needs" for relief or pleasure consume us, and we become blind to the needs of those around us. We may even begin to see them as threats.

We can break out of this cycle by opening our hearts: by being present for, and in service to, other people. Generosity allows space to respond to those around us, to include their well-being in our choices. This can, of course, be a tricky concept for those of us who struggle with issues of codependency. Generosity does not mean giving of ourselves without boundaries until we are depleted. It does not mean using "helping" as a form of manipulation to get what we want. Again, what's important here is that we're honest about the *intention* behind our actions.

We try not to confuse intention with impact. Our intention may be to not harm, but sometimes the impact is that we hurt someone. Many of us have experienced this in our addictions. Without intending to, and often without even being aware of it, we've created wreckage in other people's lives. The way we choose to practice compassion in recovery is by being accountable when our actions hurt someone, and by acknowledging this hurt without blame or shame, defensiveness or justification.

Generosity allows us to cultivate **appreciative joy,** which is one of the four **heart practices** of Buddhism, along with compassion, lovingkindness, and equanimity. Joyful appreciation is simply being happy when somebody else has good fortune, happiness, and peacefulness. Generosity lets us appreciate the happiness of others rather than having feelings of envy, jealousy, or wanting them to be just a bit less happy so we seem a little more happy by comparison. We want the other person's happiness to increase, for them to become more at peace, and so we learn to appreciate those things in their lives. In the moment of giving, of generosity, we've let go of self-centered desire and grasping what is "mine," or what brings me pleasure. We're giving up any ill-will or aversion we feel toward the person and toward the world. Instead of creating separation and withdrawal, we're actively fostering appreciation for the closeness and connectedness of the world.

This is a joy that's not weighed down by selfish desires, envy, or resentment. It's the purity of happiness for someone else's good fortune. We can choose to cultivate this feeling of joy in the happiness and success of others, without the need to compete or compare. It's actually a feeling that's natural to humans, but it's often neglected when our attention is focused on selfish craving. This is the true seat of generosity: delighting in the happiness of others, without needing anything in return.

The second heart practice is **compassion**, which is first of all a willingness to come close to pain: to recognize it, honor it, acknowledge it, and respond to it wisely. This isn't easy, because just as we want to run from or suppress our own pain, we also want to avoid being with the pain of others. Compassion means sitting with our own pain *and* that of others. It stops the cruelty of indifference. Compassion for ourselves is crucial. Self-compassion is the key to healing the shame and guilt that we often feel as we begin to recognize the harms we caused through our addictions.

Compassion is not just offering sympathy and a helping hand. It's also an intention to avoid causing harm to others and ourselves. This is where we can most easily see the difference between skillful and unskillful actions, and between wholesome and unwholesome intentions. Cruelty—and all the harm it creates in the world—comes from a lack of compassion. Cruelty is a desire to cause pain. Compassion is caring about the welfare and happiness of others. Compassion rests on the renunciation of harming living beings and is not only the wish, but also the intention to put an end to their suffering. We need to open our hearts—not just our minds—to all the suffering that is here, that is experienced in the world. Compassion is not only a feeling: it is an action.

The third heart practice is **lovingkindness**, also known as *metta*. These are thoughts that are free from ill-will, simply wishing that somebody else be happy, that they be well, and free from suffering. It's the choice to include the well-being of everyone in how we act in the world. Metta isn't conditional: it isn't something we offer only to people we like. We can have concern and care even when we're feeling our own pain. We can bring metta to mind when we're faced with difficulty or torn by conflicting feelings about the conditions of life at the moment. Metta doesn't depend on people acting in a certain way, on our feeling a certain way in the moment, or on the result of our caring. It frees us from only caring about the well-being of others when we think it will lead to some outcome. With metta, we don't ask the question "Will it do any good to care about this person's well-being?"

This means that how we think about another person isn't based on their behavior, or even on the other person at all. How we think about a person is up to us—and if it's shaped by the practice of metta, then we can care about every person's well-being, even the most difficult and unpleasant people we know. We can honestly hope that everyone finds a way to be happy without causing harm. Wishing this goodwill towards others frees us from the reactivity and anger that can come when we focus on the person's behavior or what we think they "ought" to do. We can begin to see the suffering and pain that somebody experiences as a result of their actions, and care about that pain even if it might also lead to pain for us or for others. Our wish is that all beings are free from pain and suffering, that they escape hatred and fear, that they are at ease, and that they find happiness.

Generosity, compassion, and lovingkindness make **forgiveness** not only possible, but also essential for recovery. Forgiveness rests on understanding and caring about the pain and confusion that give rise to actions that we experience as harmful. We forgive when we focus on the person, rather than the action. And we forgive only in the present when our hurt and anger make us aware that our resentment is blocking our own compassionate and generous responses. In this way, forgiveness is not so much something we are giving to the person who hurt us, but something we give to ourselves. It's centered more on our own conscious intention in how we choose to respond to them. Just as we sometimes act out of fear, greed, or confusion, we see that others do so, too. Forgiveness doesn't mean we accept or tolerate harm. It comes from understanding and accepting that the person causing us harm is doing so from a place of pain and confusion. We extend compassion and goodwill to that person, even as we actively try to end the harm. This may mean creating safe boundaries or removing ourselves from exposure to harm. But we do this from a place of compassion and understanding, not resentment.

And it is *essential* that we extend the healing of forgiveness and compassion to ourselves. Forgiveness allows us to let go of the guilt and shame of our own harmful actions. We remember that compassion is an action, so when we forgive ourselves we also set an intention not to re-create or continue the harm we have caused to others and to ourselves.

Making amends is an important part of forgiveness. As we begin to gain clarity about the harm we caused in our addiction, we commit to make amends for that harmful behavior. We don't make amends for the sake of satisfying some external standard of morality, to be forgiven, or to get something in return. Instead, we use the process as a way to let go of our expectations and disappointments in others and ourselves—in other words, to let go of our attachment to a different past.

One of the central principles of karma is that I alone am responsible for the way my past actions impact my *current* responses to the world. We change our habits by letting go of the past and restoring balance in our relationships. Things we did in the past create patterns of behavior that continue to shape our thoughts and intentions in the present. That process doesn't stop until we change our relationship with those patterns, and toward the people we've harmed. Amends are about restoring the balance in our relationships, not about asking for forgiveness from others. In a sense, it is an action we take to forgive ourselves.

When we have come to understand and face the reality of our impact on others, we begin to understand the purpose of making amends. Our compassion practice leads to a desire to relieve the suffering of people we've harmed, and a commitment to not cause further suffering. Even if the person isn't a part of our lives any longer, it's possible to acknowledge their hurt and to offer them our goodwill and our remorse. Making amends means we do what we can to remedy the harm or wrong. If that is not possible, we resolve to do some good, not as compensation, but to develop our habits in a different direction. When we intentionally take responsibility for our actions, we let go of harmful avoidance and self-judgment and develop a sense of connectedness, peace, and ease. The starting place for amends is a willingness to forgive ourselves and take the path of reconciliation: not only with those we have harmed, but also with our own hearts and minds.

Generosity, compassion, lovingkindness, and forgiveness allow us to experience **equanimity** as we face pain and discomfort, both in ourselves and others. Equanimity is the fourth of the heart practices. During our addictions, we often responded to situations that caused us anger, fear, or resentment with a craving that the situations be different. We gave up and surrendered to the negative experience of life. Equanimity does not mean giving up; it is more a quality of giving *in*. It is finding peace exactly where we are, regardless of external circumstances. Equanimity allows us to be right in the middle of things, to understand and accept things as they are without needing to escape. When we gave up, we said, "I don't care what happens." Equanimity, on the other hand, is being able to say, "I can be present for this." It's the acceptance that while there are some things we cannot change, we still have power over how we respond to them. While we don't always have control over our thoughts and feelings, we do have power over how we feed them.

Questions for Inquiry of Wise Intention:

During your periods of addictive behavior, how did you act in ways that were clinging, uncaring, harsh, cruel, or unforgiving? Toward whom (including yourself) were these feelings directed? How might generosity, compassion, lovingkindness, and forgiveness have changed your behavior?

What actions have you taken that have harmed others?

Have you formed an intention to reconcile with both yourself and the person or people you've harmed (to make amends)? If so, have you found a wise friend or mentor you can go to for guidance and support in the amends process, which is summarized below? What support can this person provide as you begin the process of amends?

Making Amends:

- Have you done something intentionally that you now recognize caused harm to another? Who has been harmed by your actions?

- Have you honestly formed the intention not to repeat harmful actions and to learn from the experience in future interactions? Have you begun the process of directly addressing the harmful actions of your past?

- Making amends depends on the circumstance, including your present relationship to the person and the extent to which you can undo the harm caused through direct actions (like correcting a public dishonesty or compensating another for things you have taken that were not freely offered). Ask yourself, "What can I do in the present?"

- Can you address and reconcile with the harm you have caused without forming an attachment to being forgiven? Identify the motivation for making each amends.

- What actions would restore balance in your own feelings and approach to whatever harm you have caused? Can these steps be taken without causing new harm to the person or the relationship?

If you're experiencing a difficult situation o
your life right now, investigate the intention
bringing to this situation.

- Are you being selfish or self-seeking?
- Are you being driven by aversion (run away from an unpleasant experience) c. craving (grasping for pleasure)? How?
- How could you bring in a spirit of generosity, compassion, lovingkindness, appreciative joy, and forgiveness to this situation?
- How would this situation look different if you brought these factors to mind *before* reacting or responding?
- If you don't want to, can you at least have the intention and willingness to do so?

Wise Speech

Wise Speech is based on the intention to do no harm. We've all used speech in a manner that may create harm: lying to keep others from knowing what's really going on; gossiping with the intention of putting someone down or satisfying our desire to be recognized; "stealing" time and attention by chattering on and on; or trying to convince others to meet our own needs at the expense of their own. Wise Speech includes all the ways we use our voices, including in writing and online.

The most basic foundation of Wise Speech is honesty or truthfulness. Dishonesty is not just outright lies; it can also take the form of exaggeration, minimizing, or omitting, all with the intention of presenting a false picture or distorting what something actually is. It can take the form of "white lies" to avoid embarrassment or exposure, half-truths to keep from being caught, or seemingly harmless things said at the expense of others.

may say more than we really know to be true in the hopes of appearing smarter or more confident in our position or feeling. Sometimes we say something before we know the truth.

Dishonesty has to do with our intention in speech–are we motivated by greed, fear, or confusion? Or are we motivated by a sincere desire to express what's true, what's useful, what's kind, and what's timely? Wise Speech means we speak with the intention of not causing harm, and of fostering safety and security in our community.

In active addiction, we develop the habit of dishonesty. We lie to cover up or mislead others about the nature and extent of our using and behavior. We lie so we can satisfy the craving our fixation feeds, by hiding our actions, our feelings, or the amount of money and effort we put into satisfying our craving. Many of us lie just for the sake of lying—because the truth represents a reality we can't tolerate. We get trapped by our secrets, and for many of us, having a double life becomes an addiction all its own. This is why honesty is foundational to recovery. Dishonesty is one of the habits that allow our addictive behaviors to flourish. As a result, recovery needs to start with an honest appraisal of exactly what lies we told and what dishonesty we spread during our addictive behavior.

The Buddha provided some guidelines for Wise Speech, in addition to truthfulness. He said to avoid slander and gossip, recognizing that such unwise speech causes conflict and makes the community less safe. So, when we talk about others, we can ask ourselves: What's our intention? Is it to cause division or exclusion? Is it to cause shame or embarrassment in someone else, or to somehow make ourselves look better at somebody else's expense? It's possible to talk about other people with the intention of kindness, generosity, and compassion, to seek understanding or support for another. Gossip and slander don't do this and instead, cause harm. Similarly, idle chatter and saying things just to be heard or recognized, or to take up time when we're uncomfortable, can lead people to dismiss or ignore us and may create impatience and intolerance in a community.

Wise Speech also involves the *tone* we use when we talk. If we express ourselves in harsh, angry, or abusive ways, we may not be heard even if we're being truthful. Speaking gently, with the intention of kindness, fosters a community of friendliness and safety.

It may sound like Wise Speech is primarily about discerning when *not* to speak, but this isn't always the case. Many of us grew up in families where it wasn't safe to talk openly about our thoughts and feelings. Some, because of certain experiences or cultural conditioning, have been taught that we don't have permission to use our voices. For many of us, practicing Wise Speech may mean learning how to use our voices that have been silenced, how to wisely communicate the needs and boundaries we've gotten used to keeping hidden. Many of us, in an effort to be liked or for fear of rocking the boat, have favored being nice over being honest and true to ourselves. But Wise Speech teaches us that speaking up, even when it's hard, is sometimes the wise choice, and that speech is never truly kind if we cause harm to ourselves.

A final part of Wise Speech is careful listening. We must listen with compassion, understanding, and receptivity. It can be really helpful to observe how much of the time we spend "listening" to someone else is actually spent judging them or planning what we're going to say in response. Deep listening—without selfishness, or an agenda—is an act of generosity that lets us build true connection.

Have you caused harm with your speech? How?

Have you been dishonest or harsh in your communication? When, and in what specific ways?

Do you use speech now to hurt or control people, to present a false idea or image of yourself or of reality, to demand attention, or to relieve the discomfort of silence? Detail specific instances in which you used speech to mislead, misdirect, or distract.

Are you careful to avoid causing harm with your speech?

Do you say things you know are not true, or pretend to know the truth about something when you don't, to appear more knowledgeable or credible than you are? List some examples.

Wise Action

Wise Action is also based in the intention to do no harm and to foster compassion, lovingkindness, generosity, and forgiveness. We try to do what's skillful, and avoid actions that are unskillful. Wise Action asks that we try to make choices based on understanding and not unthinking habits or ignorance.

The Buddha suggested that we make a commitment to avoid five specific actions that cause harm, a commitment which is known as the **Five Precepts**. We commit to the Five Precepts as our basic ethical system:

1. We set the intention to avoid taking the life of another living being, or from causing harm to ourselves or another living being.
2. We set the intention to avoid taking what is not freely given, or stealing.

3. We set the intention to avoid causing harm though our sexual conduct, and to be aware of the consequences and impact of our sexual activity and desire.
4. We set the intention of being honest, of not lying, and of not using speech in a harmful way.
5. We set the intention to avoid the use of intoxicants and intoxicating behavior that cloud our awareness.

We need to continually reflect on and question the intentions behind our actions. We may have moments of clarity, but these can quickly pass, when old habits or thinking resurfaces. We commit to constantly reminding ourselves of our intention to Wise Action: to act in ways that are non-harming.

Questions for Inquiry of Wise Action:

Have you acted in a way that was unskillful or that created suffering? How?

During those times you were unskillful or created suffering, how would it have changed the outcome if you had acted out of compassion, kindness, generosity, and forgiveness? Would you now have a different emotional or mental response to your past actions if you had acted with these principles in mind?

First Precept:

- Have you caused harm? How?
  (Allow for a broad understanding of harm, including physical, emotional, mental, and karmic harm as well as financial, legal, moral, or other forms of harm.)
- Even if you can't point to specific harms that you have caused, have you acted in a way that purposely avoided being aware of the possibility of harm?

Second Precept:

- People "take" in many ways: we take goods or material possessions, we take time and energy, we take care and recognition. With this broad understanding of taking, have you taken what has not been freely given? How? What are specific examples or patterns where this has been true for you?

Third Precept:

- Have you behaved irresponsibly, selfishly, or without full consent and awareness (from yourself or partners) in your sexual conduct? How?
- Reviewing your sexual partners or activities, have you been fully aware in each instance of other existing relationships, prior or current mental or emotional conditions of yourself and your partner(s), and your own intentions in becoming sexually involved? How or how not?
- Has your sexual activity, both by yourself and with others, been based on non-harmful intentions? Have you entered into each sexual activity with awareness and understanding? How or how not?

Fourth Precept:

- Have you been dishonest? How?
- What patterns did your dishonesty take? Did you act or speak dishonestly to deny or misrepresent the truth about your own behavior or status?
- Were there particular situations in which your dishonesty was particularly present (for instance: when dealing with your addictive behaviors, in job or professional settings, among friends, with family)? Investigate the source of the dishonesty in each setting: Was it based on greed, confusion, fear, denial? Why were you lying?

Fifth Precept:

- Have you used intoxicants or other behaviors that cloud your ability to see clearly?
- What substances and behaviors have you become reliant on to change or cloud your awareness? Has this changed over time? Or, if you have periods of abstinence, were your habitual intoxicants or behaviors replaced by other ways to avoid awareness of your present circumstances and conditions? How?

List ways you might practice the Five Precepts, compassion, lovingkindness, and generosity in your decision-making.

Wise Livelihood

The final factor in the ethical group is Wise Livelihood, which focuses on how we support ourselves in the world. Again, the intent is to avoid causing harm. For most of us, our work occupies so much of our time and attention, so how we choose to make a living takes on special importance. Understanding the principle of karma, and knowing that unwholesome activity gives rise to unwholesome karma, whatever choices or circumstances lead us to a particular job need to be recognized as having karmic consequences.

We try to avoid jobs that give rise to suffering, and seek work that does no harm or reduces suffering. The Buddha mentions five kinds of livelihood to avoid: trading in weapons or instruments of killing, trafficking in or selling human beings, killing of other beings, making or selling addictive drugs, or business in poison. We're encouraged to avoid occupations based on dishonesty or injury.

Whatever our job is, we can practice it mindfully, with an intention of non-harm, of easing suffering, and of compassion. This means developing an attitude toward our occupation beyond just the money we make. We can develop an approach of service and caring about the effects of our actions on others, both within and outside our workspaces. Wise Livelihood is not about judging ourselves or others for their choice of work or trying to limit their choices. Instead, we try to understand why and how we engage in whatever occupation we practice. Whatever work we do, we can maintain an intention of benefiting others.

Questions for Inquiry of Wise Livelihood:

Does your job cause harm? What is the specific nature of that harm?

How can you do your job more mindfully and with an intention of compassion and non-harm?

Do you bring an understanding of karma and kindness to your job, or do you compartmentalize it and exclude it from awareness of wise action?

What part does greed play in the choices you make in your livelihood? Does greed get in the way of awareness or compassion?

How can you be of more service in your community?

How might you bring a spirit of generosity to your life, both in your profession and outside it?

Wise Effort

Wise Effort is the first of the concentration group. It means concentrating our effort on understanding and recovery and awakening. Wise Effort isn't based on how *much* we should meditate, how *much* service we should do, or how *much* time we put into healthy activity. Instead, it's the intention to devote balanced energy to supporting the other parts of the path, particularly wisdom.

The first thing to pay attention to is avoiding situations and states of mind that can lead to unwholesome, unskillful, or harmful responses. We become more aware of conditions in our lives, and investigate our own responses and reactions to those conditions. When we're operating out of greed, ignorance, confusion, or thinking we can get what we want, we need to be aware of that.

We put in the effort and energy to understand what circumstances allowed these conditions to arise and how we can begin to move away from those responses.

Energy or effort is also devoted to letting compassion, lovingkindness, generosity, and forgiveness arise when they're *not* present. If we find ourselves reacting with anger rather than compassion, fear instead of generosity, blame instead of forgiveness, we can ask how we would respond if those positive factors were present, and begin to respond more skillfully. Being hard on ourselves, beating ourselves up, and suffering from perfectionism are all familiar feelings during addiction and recovery. When we shame ourselves for not being good enough, not trying hard enough, not being enough, these are perfect opportunities to practice Wise Effort, to reflect on the question, "In this moment, how can I be kind and gentle with myself?"

In early recovery, we may be most interested in damage control: simply stopping the destruction and demoralization we have suffered through our habitual, unskillful responses to craving. We can begin by awareness of that craving, and learning to make different choices that don't trigger the craving. Sometimes awareness is enough; sometimes that's all the effort we can muster. As we learn more skillful responses to our triggers, we gain space to have more compassion, lovingkindness, generosity, and forgiveness. And as this practice becomes more of a habit, equanimity and peacefulness begin to replace our habits of grasping and selfishness. Pacing ourselves is important, alternating periods of activity and rest. We need to be aware of what our mind, emotions, body, and recovery can handle *right now,* and avoid the stress that can come from pushing ourselves too far, too fast. We need to avoid those things that put us into unskillful mind-states, and try to do things that return us to a more easeful way of being in the present moment.

Try to remember that whatever your experience is right now, it will pass, often in unpredictable ways. Remind yourself that you don't really know how long an unpleasant or painful experience will last. Try to be open to recognizing and investigating the experience while it is present, without interpreting it as a permanent part of your experience. Recognizing that the craving, experience, or thought will pass makes it easier to avoid the impulse to make an immediate, unskillful response.

Questions for Inquiry of Wise Effort:

What efforts have you made to connect with a wise friend, mentor, or dharma buddy who can help you develop and balance your efforts?

Think of a situation that is causing you discomfort or unease. What is the nature of the effort you're bringing to the situation? Pay attention to whether it feels balanced and sustainable, or if you're leaning too far in the direction of either inactivity or overexertion?

Are you dealing with overwhelming desires, aversions, laziness or discouragement, restlessness and worry, or doubt about your own ability to recover? How do these hindrances affect the choices you're making?

Are you avoiding feelings by checking out and giving up, or through obsessive busyness and perfectionism?

Wise Mindfulness

Mindfulness—being present to what's going on in our minds, bodies, hearts, and world—is central to the practice of the Eightfold Path. We learn to be present for the way things are with compassion, without judging them or ourselves. Mindfulness is being aware of whatever is present, noticing it, and letting it pass. It's also remembering that we're on a path leading to our freedom and long-lasting happiness.

Mindfulness asks us to be aware and to investigate, without the reactivity and grasping for control that leads to suffering. We learn to stay attentive to what's happening without having to either react to *or* deny what's happening. For many of us, our addictions prevented us from being mindful. In fact, that was often the whole point: we used our substances and behaviors to avoid feeling, to avoid being aware, because being aware was painful. But by trying to avoid pain, we often created more suffering. We're now making a different choice—to sit with the discomfort rather than pushing it away or trying to numb it. We can learn to sit with the discomfort in different ways, either up close and personal (saying "This fear is simply a bunch of body sensations") or in a more distant, non-attached way ("There's the fear and I don't have to let it control me"). We're choosing to respond to it with mindful investigation and compassion, and to trust that it will pass if we let it. We're remembering that there's another way to respond to life.

Our minds can get lost in how we react to experiences. When something happens, we almost immediately begin to create a story, plan, or fantasy about it. We have a thought about an experience, that thought leads to another, and on and on until we're far from a real understanding of the experience itself. Mindfulness is noticing the experience in that moment *before* we get lost in the judgment of the moment or the stories we spin about it. Rather than blindly following our reactions and responses to an experience, mindfulness allows us the space to choose to respond skillfully and from a place of wisdom and morality.

Mindfulness encourages us to be open to and investigate the painful experiences (and our habitual reactions to those experiences), rather than to deny, ignore, suppress, or run from them. Most of us have been conditioned to be our own harshest critic from early on, especially during our fixations on substances and behaviors. We carry the shadow of that judge with us, even as we seek recovery, giving ourselves negative feedback and scrutinizing every effort we make, holding ourselves to impossible standards of perfection. Letting go of that inner critic allows us to be mindful in the present of the efforts we are making, mindful of the compassion and lovingkindness we're learning to make a part of our practice and our lives. Remember that we often talk *way* more harshly to ourselves than we ever would to somebody else. It's useful to notice when we're treating ourselves too harshly, and then shift attention to what we are doing well. We can acknowledge the negative thought, and then gently let it go.

Mindfulness practice is based on what are called the **four foundations**. The first foundation, **mindfulness of the body**, asks us to bring awareness, attention, or focus to breathing and to bodily sensations. Meditations on the breath and body are focused on this awareness. The second foundation is **mindfulness of feeling and feeling tones**. This practice involves noticing the emotional tone—pleasure or displeasure—that comes with every sensation, even when the sensation is a thought. It also encourages us to notice when a sensation is neither pleasant nor unpleasant but feels neutral. For example, we can experience the sensations of breathing–the sensation of breathing in, the sensation of exhaling–by noticing where in our body we feel the breath most directly. But we can experience the sensations without feeling particular pleasure in the sensations of breathing: breathing is just there, it's a natural process of being alive. The second foundation instructs us to notice those sensations that are neutral, as well as those that are pleasant or unpleasant.

The third foundation, **mindfulness of the mind**, asks us to notice when attachment—also known as greed or want-ing—comes up, and to be aware that the attachment arises in the mind. We also learn to notice when the mind is not attached to a particular thought or sensation. The same practice of noticing applies when we become aware of aversion, which we can experience as resistance or even hatred. And, when aversion isn't present in the mind, we notice that the mind is free from aversion.

In the fourth foundation of mind-fulness, **mindfulness of mental objects** (or of mental phenomena), we begin to simply notice when a thought arises, being aware of it without judgment or evaluation, and allowing it to pass away without holding onto it and without creating a story out of it. Training in the fourth foundation lets us be aware of thoughts arising and passing away, and that each thought will pass if we allow it to.

Two simple practices can make mindfulness more a part of our daily lives. First, we can stop whatever we're doing at any moment, and pay attention to the physical sensation of three in-breaths and three out-breaths. This simple practice grounds our attention in what's present right now, rather than in the voices and critics we carry with us. Shifting from the stories and judgments we constantly create during the day to this simple grounding practice of three breaths gives us the space we sometimes need to return to mindfulness of the present.

A second practice is to take time to inquire into the truthfulness of the negative or difficult messages we give ourselves. First, take time to ask yourself whether the message is true. Second, ask how sure you are that it's true. Are you absolutely certain about what may seem like an easy or automatic truth? Third, notice how you feel when you believe the thought: Does it lead to fear, anger, sadness, desire? Finally, reflect on who you'd be without the thought. How would you feel if you weren't caught up in the particular mindset or scenario you're creating?

Questions for Inquiry of Wise Mindfulness:

What are steps you can take to support a regular meditation practice?

What are steps you can take to practice mindfulness more throughout the day by checking in with yourself about how you're feeling, and pausing before reacting to situations?

What are steps you can take to sit with your discomfort instead of running from it or running toward temporary pleasure?

What are steps you can take to question the "truths" that your mind tells you, rather than automatically believing them? Identify specific instances where your mind and perceptions "lied" to you about the truth of a situation, and how being aware of that might have changed your reaction and led to a less harmful outcome.

Think about times when you felt fear, doubt, or hesitation. Now, let yourself become aware of their temporary nature. How might that awareness have led to an outcome that was less harmful?

Wise Concentration

The final aspect of the Eightfold Path is Wise Concentration. Meditation practice begins with concentrating on the breath, the body, the emotional tone of the moment, and the processes of the mind itself, because these things exist in the present. If we focus on breath, for example, we're paying attention to the present moment because our breathing is immediate: it's happening *right now*. Breathing is a natural process that doesn't require judgment or interpretation, and so it eases the mind from the need to react.

The purpose of concentration is to train the mind to be focused and undistracted. This circles back to the wisdom section, where we try to be focused on wise understanding and wise thought, without being distracted by habitual perceptions and reactivity.

Most of us, early in meditation practice, are distracted by things around us. Our concentration is interrupted by a noise outside the room, a pain or discomfort in our bodies, our own worries or judgments of the experience, boredom or weariness, or thoughts and plans. These distractions can lead to a feeling of unease or restlessness. This is perfectly normal. In our addictions, we nurtured the habit of distracting ourselves; for many of us, it has become a survival technique. Concentration meditation gives us the opportunity to meet this habit with kindness and patience rather than resistance.

Concentration, like the rest of the factors of the Eightfold Path, is a practice. As with any practice, it takes time and effort to learn a new way to focus attention. In meditation, simply noting the distraction, accepting that it exists, and then refocusing, *is* the practice. If we become consumed with discomfort, thoughts, or distraction, we need to first recognize that it's happening, and then become curious about it. Then we can make the choice to refocus—to concentrate on the object of the meditation. Our habitual patterns can seduce us into thinking we're doing it wrong, into judging our practice, or into giving up. Don't let them. When we observe what the mind is telling us and react with compassion, knowing we have the power to recognize it and refocus it, we strengthen our ability to concentrate.

Concentration can be especially helpful in times of craving. Instead of getting lost in the delusion that we must have what we're craving, we can trust that the craving is only temporary and refocus our attention on our intention to act wisely. This may simply be the three-breath pause mentioned earlier, or a more formal sitting meditation concentrating on the breath. We can use concentration meditation to train our minds to focus on a wholesome thought in the midst of temporary discomfort and the yearning for a quick fix. This may take the form of repeated phrases to focus and clear the mind, such as metta, compassion, or equanimity meditations. For some of us, this may take the form of prayer, a self-affirmation, a mantra, or another form of focused attention. Concentration practices can often bring a sense of well-being and peace in a time of turmoil. They're a healthy way to return to a balanced, resilient state when we're stressed or agitated.

Sometimes when cravings or unpleasant emotions are particularly strong, moving the body can be the best way to help refocus our energy and find relief. Concentration at those times may mean being focused and mindful about each movement we are making: *this is my foot taking a step, this is my hand reaching for the cup*. After a few minutes of concentration practice, of not giving energy to our craving or obsession, we may find the intensity of the feeling has passed. The more we do this, the more we gain confidence that we have the power to relieve the suffering of our addiction through following this path and committing to this practice.

For trauma survivors, the breath, the heart, and the mind can be potentially overwhelming places to place the attention. So if traditional anchors like breath and body are challenging, ask yourself: What helps you stay present? What helps to calm your nervous system? It might be the floor in front of you, or a statue, or a piece of art on the wall. It might even be just a blank wall. All that you need to be present is to pay attention to something happening right now.

If you do feel powerful emotions begin to arise during meditation, there are some simple things you can do to remain present. For example, you can open your eyes rather than keeping them closed, or give yourself permission to back off from the practice you are working on. Do whatever you need to do to take care of yourself should such a state arise, whether that is taking some deep breaths, putting a name on your experience (such as "flashback"), or silently repeating some compassionate phrases to yourself.

Learning to turn our attention back and forth between challenging sensations and our own supportive resources is a valuable skill that professionals call *titration*. You can be gentle with your practice as you are working to develop this skill.

Questions for Inquiry of Wise Concentration:

How do you get unfocused or distracted in meditation?

What distracts you the most?

What are steps you can take to refocus your mind without judging your own practice?

Notice what value or learning you could gain by carefully and kindly noticing where your mind has gone, or what has distracted you.

What are steps you can take to use concentration to see clearly and act wisely?

What are steps you can take to be kind and gentle with yourself through this process?

Community: *Sangha*

Sangha is the third of the Three Jewels: loosely translated, it means "community." It's where Buddha and Dharma find their expression, where we're supported in putting those principles into action. It's a community of friends practicing the dharma together in order to develop our own awareness and maintain it. The traditional definition of sangha originally described monastic communities of ordained monks and nuns, but in many Buddhist traditions it has evolved to include the wider spiritual community. For us, our sangha is our community of both dharma practice and recovery.

We are decentralized and leaderless, and there are no rules to follow other than that the meeting should be an open, safe, and accessible space that tries to uphold our core principles of mindfulness, compassion, forgiveness, and generosity. The advice in this chapter comes from the collective experience of hundreds of local groups, and so it's offered in the spirit of friendly guidance rather than direction.

The essence of a sangha is awareness, understanding, acceptance, harmony, integrity, and lovingkindness. Recovery begins when we learn to pay attention to and investigate experience in the present moment. It's through the sangha that we first learn to be fully present—that we stop trying to satisfy our craving and turn to an understanding of our thoughts, feelings, sense experience, and actions that includes others. This understanding is fundamentally *relational*. Our actions have consequences on not only our own lives, but also on the people we meet and share experiences with. Many of us learned this the hard way—by hurting the ones we loved while we were in active addiction. A core part of our recovery includes making amends to those we have hurt, including ourselves. As we've seen, our recovery includes the wise intention to heal the suffering we have caused others and to act wisely to avoid creating the same suffering in the future.

Sangha provides the opportunity to practice a central part of recovery: *remembering*. Remembering means the wholesome reflection that supports us in our recovery, and energizes our practice of compassion, lovingkindness, generosity, and forgiveness. Sharing these experiences with others who are also struggling with addictive behaviors helps give us confidence in our own ability to recover our true nature, our potential for awakening. Sangha enlarges our perspective and begins to give us the self-confidence and self-respect that will let us reflect on the ups and downs of recovery without discouragement or hopelessness. When we feel inspired to practice with wise friends, we can trust them to point out when we fall short of our intentions, and we can be honest with ourselves.

The teachings of the Buddha clearly state, over and over again, that this is not just something we can do on our own. And many programs of recovery (including our own) stress the importance of going to meetings and working with others in recovery. This is often something we resist, and not without reason: some meetings are boring; some ask us to believe things that we feel are untrue; some are depressing or intimidating or unwelcoming for a lot of reasons. But it's with the support of others that so many of us have found relief from the suffering and isolation brought on by our addictions. And it's through being of service that we've been able to get out of our own heads and experience a more sustainable and wholesome joy than our addictions provided.

Many of us have found that there's a quality to our meditations that's different when practiced with a group. Particularly when we're getting started, it can be easy to give up or space out after a few minutes. Practicing with others can often give us the motivation to stick with it long enough to start experiencing some of the benefits of practice. And through sharing our experience and listening to what others have to say, we can see how we're not alone in a lot of our challenges. This can come as a welcome surprise after years of suffering shame and feeling like an outcast.

Many of us, having habitually isolated ourselves, have found that sharing silence at a meeting creates an atmosphere of trust and can be a calming way to get used to being with others. No one is required to speak or participate in meetings: passing is always an option when it comes time to share. There's never any requirement to believe in anything, to identify yourself in any way, much less to become a Buddhist or serious practitioner. The wisdom and tools are available to everyone, wherever they are on their path.

But not every meeting is going to be a fit for every person. You may live in an area where there are several different options to choose from, or there may be only a single recovery meeting near you, or none at all. Fortunately, there are also online meetings, many of which can be joined by phone. You can also start your own meeting.

However you find them, trust that there are wise friends and a sangha out there for you.

Isolation and Connection

Addiction and addictive behavior can create people without roots. Some of us have been uprooted from our families and from society. We wander around, feeling as though we're not quite whole, because our addictions feed our isolation and loneliness. Many come from broken families and feel rejected by society or have been isolated from society through incarceration or institutionalization. Not all of us have disassociated to that degree, but we do tend to live on the margins, looking for a home, for something to belong to. A community of practice—a sangha—can provide a second chance to someone who's become alienated from society, or just a comfortable place to bring all of ourselves, including parts we don't usually share with others. If the community of practice is organized with a friendly, warm atmosphere, we can find support for our practice and recovery.

In our addictions, we self-medicated or engaged in behaviors that helped us deal with the pain of separation. The relief was temporary, of course, often leaving us more lonely and isolated than before, yet we returned to it again and again. For many of us, it was the only way we knew to relieve the pain. Even in sobriety, when faced with well-meaning but insistent people telling us how to overcome our addictions, the instinct for many of us is to keep to ourselves. It's a habitual way of being in the world that a lot of us share.

It wasn't just getting high, though for a lot of people in this fellowship and outside it, that was the main road we took to escape. There were other traps that snagged us, even if we never struggled with substances: sex, food, self-harm, social media. We may have tried to get help with those compulsions, but often found others minimizing or trivializing them, especially in comparison to drug or alcohol abuse. For those of us whose primary addictions are around behaviors and processes, we may have felt alienated and excluded from recovery itself.

Many of us found ourselves like raw, exposed nerves when we stopped using those ways to escape. And sometimes, the last place we wanted to be was in a room with strangers in a circle of chairs all facing each other, talking about how we can't drink or use or participate in our destructive behaviors anymore. The paradox is that it's in that kind of space, where we're accepted as we are, that we can begin to let go of our reflex to hide.

Many of us lost the ability, if we ever had it, to form relationships without the social lubricant of alcohol or drugs. Sometimes that was because we dealt with rejection, trauma, or loss at an early age and became anxious and avoidant around others. Or maybe we just felt different than everyone else since the day we were born, or came from a small community (or a big family) and got sick of people nosing into our business. Whatever reasons we had to isolate, we got to a point where it stopped serving us. The substances and behaviors we used to protect ourselves began to harm ourselves and others. We drove people away to be safe, and as a result we became even more lonely.

Some of us learned to isolate for good reason. People we loved and trusted harmed us in terrible ways. Some of us lived in communities and families where we constantly felt unsafe, where trusting anybody too much could be costly. In recovery, we're making the scary, difficult, and brave decision to try it out again.

All humans are driven from birth to seek close human contact. When we're deprived of it and even begin to lose the ability to find it, we suffer and become vulnerable to craving and addictive behavior. The mindfulness techniques and insights that the Buddha taught are key to recovering this ability. But it's not something we have to do alone. In fact, having people to help and support us on the path is an integral part of the teachings. So, as it turns out, the solution and the way to get to the solution are actually one and the same.

A lot of us are perennial outsiders. We've felt—often with some justification—that we have been failed and abandoned by schools, by religious institutions or the government, and often by our own families. As a result, we came to mistrust organizations and groups, and even the idea of belonging itself. The double-bind there, of course, is that because we never allow anyone to get to know us, we cut off the possibility of ever belonging.

The Buddha taught that nothing and nobody exists on its own. He said: "Since this exists, that exists, and since this does not exist, that does not exist." We're connected to other people through the way we interact, through the air we share, through our existence together in nature. Trying to ignore or resist this interconnection is basically trying to destroy something which already exists.

This doesn't mean that we're *literally* dependent on others for our life and our existence, but that the life and existence of everybody and everything develops through their relationships with things outside themselves: the food they eat, the environment they live in, the history and the circumstances of their world. It's a great web of being that each of us is connected to without any effort of our own. And being aware of that connection gives us space to have meaningful and positive relationships with others. It is a choice that each of us has: to decide what we want to do with the reality of our connection.

Sangha, in a very broad sense, means being willing to let other people in, to let them matter. To do that, we have to be willing for other people to let *us* in. When we can even consider the possibility of that happening, there's the potential for us to move toward liberation. And the benefits are felt almost immediately.

All of us, during our development and experience of life, had experiences that make us doubt our own "voice," or the value or wisdom of expressing that voice. Many of these doubts contributed to the suffering we experienced during addiction and continue to make it difficult to connect to our own recovery. Our meetings are intended as places where we can feel safe and comfortable authentically expressing what we really feel and experience. However, many of us, because of prior experience and experiences in both social settings and in the recovery community, struggle with this a lot; we often struggle just to understand our feelings and experiences.

The sangha allows us to start to explore the ways we can find and authentically express our voices, to value our own voices, and to be sure that our voices are heard. Your recovery sangha can be one that focuses on helping and encouraging those many voices.

In the Buddhist tradition, it's not just that we don't have to do this work alone, it's that we *need* the support of others on the path to waking up. In a famous story, the Buddha's cousin and assistant Ananda came to visit him and remarked, "This is half of the holy life: having admirable people as friends, companions, and colleagues." The Buddha disagreed, saying that "having admirable people as friends, companions, and colleagues is actually the *whole* of the holy life."

When we come together to talk honestly about ourselves and what happened in our lives, something very powerful can happen. When we see people committing to be who they truly are, in all their imperfections and their longing to be free, our hearts naturally begin to open because their realness allows us to be more real. In their vulnerability, our wise, admirable friends give us the freedom to be vulnerable ourselves, and to speak our own truths. So our sangha becomes the place where we are supported and encouraged to stay on the path, even when it's challenging or our progress seems stuck. Our wise friends are, without words, telling us that if we keep going, so will they.

And often, that makes all the difference.

Working with Others

For many of us in early recovery, asking for help feels almost impossible. But we have found, as difficult as it can be, that it can literally save our lives, and that with practice, it becomes easier.

However, asking for help is not just important because it may get results. At times, in fact, it might not. Even with a lot of help and support, things can still stand in our way. Sometimes, what we want from the world and from ourselves is just more than what's available right then. However, even if asking for help may not always get us what we want, it will always help get us through. When we practice accepting help from people who are offering to help, we become just a little bit more open and a little less stuck. It's the decision to reach out, as much as the answer we receive, that can give us what we need to move forward.

Nevertheless, that decision is often a heavy lift for us. Many of us have done things during our active addictions that we're not proud of. Some of the decisions we made in the past have far-reaching consequences that continue to impact our lives even after we begin our recovery. We may have worn a mask of competence, or fearlessness, or blamelessness, and the fear of what might happen when we take the mask off may keep us from reaching out. We may be afraid that if we ask people in our lives for help with financial problems, legal trouble, or any of those sorts of issues, we might lose them. We might worry that they will no longer respect us or accept us once the mask is gone, because our fear is that we'll be revealed as broken, fundamentally flawed people. We may even be afraid that there's just *nothing* behind the mask, that we're simply empty underneath.

We practice compassion for all beings, including ourselves, to see the truth beneath those fears: that there is a loving and lovable heart within all of us. We come to see clearly that those around us feel more pain watching us struggle alone that they would if we let them in. And, of course, by shutting people out and refusing to let them see our struggles, we'll often bring about the loss and isolation that we were trying to avoid in the first place. So, in view of our own suffering and the pain we can cause to those closest to us, we can see that asking for help is not selfish. In fact, it is an act of great compassion to ourselves and others.

Those who have shared the pain of addiction and isolation understand the fear and shame better than we might imagine. Through listening at meetings and sharing our own experiences, we begin to see how we're not uniquely broken or flawed. And it's often easier to ask for help from someone other than those people you're closest with. In addition to the people in your sangha, there may be counselors and other professionals in your community who can be a resource when you need someone with experience and a greater degree of objectivity. Some clinics and universities even offer community counseling on a sliding pay scale, so you may not have to eliminate that option just for financial reasons. And if you are able to make an appointment, know that some fear and reluctance is perfectly natural, and shouldn't be a reason to cancel the session.

Of course, we know intellectually that our problems become easier to face when we have help, but emotionally we may still feel fear. Here again, it's the decision to give it a try that may be more valuable than the outcome of the meeting itself. We learn that letting people in and being a little more vulnerable is not as frightening as we may have thought. In fact, we may often find that it's less daunting than the idea of dealing with our problems all by ourselves.

When we make a practice of asking for help, we frequently find that it improves both the quantity and quality of our relationships in general. Even if you don't become personally close with people in your sangha outside of meetings, you may find that you are able to connect with more people on a deep level, and that could be something entirely new in your life. Even if you are seeking help from a clergyperson, a therapist, or some other sort of professional, notice how opening up to another person affects how much *you* trust *them*. Is there a deepening of respect and feeling of safety as your ability to be transparent grows? This confidence and security may also bring benefits to your other personal relationships. Try to notice these changes as they arise, and give yourself credit for taking steps that are often difficult.

It's pretty common to worry that sharing your problems with people will cause them to look down on you, burden them with your baggage, or even upset them in some way. And while we must be honest in acknowledging that may be a risk, we also know that remaining isolated can be a much greater risk to ourselves and to others.

In general, there is a lot of truth in the cliché that burdens are lighter when they're shared. Most of us have felt like an enormous weight has been removed from our shoulders when we made the choice to not be alone with our problems anymore. And as we experience that relief, we find that asking for help becomes easier and easier.

The truth, for many of us, is that when we first come into recovery we may not immediately have easy access to our inner wisdom. Many of us have been relying on the delusion of fear and shame and reactivity as our guides in life. It takes time to lift those veils, to dig through those layers, in order to break those habits and begin to see clearly. For many of us, it takes time to be able to trust ourselves again. But we can look to our sangha, to our community of wise friends on the path, for guidance and wisdom. When we don't know what to do, when we lose faith that we can make it through this craving, when we're lost in obsession and can't make sense of our own minds and hearts, when the world feels upside down, when we are crawling out of our skin with discomfort, when we have no idea what the next wise step is-this is when we can and must reach out to our sangha for help. Because they've gone through what we have. They've made it to the other side. And hey can show us how.

Wise Friends and Mentors

Many—if not most—recovery meetings are focused on meditating together, reading literature or exploring specific topics, and sharing. There are no requirements for attendance other than a respectful curiosity, and attending meetings are a great opportunity for newcomers to visit and learn about the program. Sometimes, those who have decided to commit to this program of recovery want more support on the path. This is where the idea of a "wise friend" or "mentor" comes in.

The Buddha talked about four kinds of friends: the helpful friend, the kind of friend who sticks with you through good times and bad, the compassionate friend, and the mentor. A **wise friend** supports us through example, kindness, and compassion. It can be anyone in the sangha who we trust to act as a guide, a supporter, a partner, or just a fellow traveler on the path. This relationship may take many forms, but it is one built on honesty, compassion, healthy boundaries, and a shared intention to support one another's recovery.

For some of us, especially newcomers, it's helpful to work with a **mentor**: a wise friend who's been following the program for a while who gives support, is there to reach out to when times get rough, and can help hold us accountable. It's not a formal position: nobody is "certified" or "authorized" to be a mentor. They are just members of the community freely sharing their journey through the Four Truths and Eightfold Path. Everybody decides for themselves if they want to collaborate with someone else on their path, understanding that they must ultimately do the work of recovery themselves. Clear communication about expectations – from *both* people – is important. There are no strict rules, but if you are asked to help someone else in this way, it's a good idea to have someone who's done it before to support you. It's also strongly encouraged that you commit to the Five Precepts, at least as far as the supportive relationship is concerned.

Many people form study or practice groups in addition to regular meetings, in order to give and receive help from wise friends on their path of recovery. Some folks call these *kalyana mitta* groups, the Pāli term for wise or admirable friends. Some call them "Dharma buddies." Whatever the name, people gather to explore particular aspects of the path in a smaller group, like practicing longer periods of sitting meditation, studying the Buddhist texts, or listening to recorded Dharma talks. There's no one way to run these sort of groups, and no special experience is needed to start one. You can experiment for yourselves, and also look at the experience of established groups for ideas.

There are also groups that have formed to support each other in writing inquiries or investigations of how their addictive behavior led to suffering. This is a powerful technique for self-discovery and liberation, and like most things in this program, there is no one "right" way to do it. Some approach it in the same way as inventories in 12-Step programs, and some don't. The goal is not to cause shame or to dwell on past traumas, but rather to turn toward the pain and confusion we have been running from and learn to meet it with kindness, forgiveness, and compassion. You may consider using the Questions for Inquiry in this book as a starting place for your own exploration, and there are also a number of other written formats available.

If you need help, know that you're a part of the broader community of wise friends: the sangha of people using Buddhism for recovery. It's strongly encouraged for at least one person in the group to have someone they can check in with about best practices and safety. Especially when we are working with difficult aspects of our pasts, holding safe space will require wisdom and compassion from all members.

At any time, in groups as well as in every aspect of our lives, the reminder is that when in doubt, we can be present and we can be kind.

Service and Generosity

Different schools of Buddhism have slightly different lists of strengths or good qualities that lead a person to enlightenment. First on every one of those lists, though, is *dāna*, or generosity. We often think of generosity in terms of money, and many groups use the word dāna to describe the donations that members give to help support the meeting. In the Buddhist tradition, though, dāna is *any* act of giving - not just money but also food, time, or our attention - without expecting anything in return. You may already be familiar with the emphasis that many recovery programs put on service, which is perfectly in line with this ancient teaching. The merit of this practice has been central to many religions and philosophies down through the centuries.

Generosity with our time, energy, and attention is not

only of benefit to others on this path. As we become more generous, it also helps us loosen the grip of greed and attachment that caused so much of our own suffering. From the first time we mindfully put a couple of dollars in the offering bowl or introduce ourselves to a newcomer after a meeting, we can start to feel the benefit of being generous without asking for thanks. In our meditation practice, we learn through direct experience how our bodies and our wealth are impermanent, and this insight makes us more willing to do good with them while we still have them. Sharing our experience at a meeting, or even simply meditating along with others and giving our silent encouragement and support, is an act of kindness that benefits both ourselves and our sangha.

Many of us have trained ourselves for years to be vigilant about being "taken advantage of" or "ripped off." In some cases, this has certainly been justified, and there will always be times where we will need to set and maintain healthy boundaries. But as our practice deepens, we're able to do so with an attitude of discernment and compassion. In the Buddhist teachings, generosity is not a commandment or a "you should," or an unrealistic standard that people are expected to measure themselves by and find themselves falling short. It is, instead, a description of our true nature, of the open and loving hearts that have always been within us, but that have been covered up for so long that they were almost lost to us. The practice helps us to recover this original nature.

As we try to be more and more generous in our meetings and in our lives, we learn to trust our own innate kindness, and we build up confidence that we can give of ourselves to others and still be safe. We continually test what we think are our limitations, and grow in self-esteem, self-respect, and well-being as we see these limitations for what they are: defensive strategies that may once have been necessary, but which have hardened into the handcuffs of habit. The voice of our attachments may say, "I don't want to put my hard-earned money in that bowl," or "Maybe I'll do this act of service, but I'll stop if people don't show enough appreciation." As we practice generosity, we see how these fears are transparent, how they have kept us small. We begin to realize that this practice is really about creating more space in our hearts and minds. As we notice our limits and allow ourselves to go beyond them, our heart-minds become more expansive, more spacious, and composed. This brings us greater feelings of happiness and self-respect, and gives our practice more strength and flexibility to look at the conditions of our lives and our recovery.

We can see the benefits of such a practice when we think about the opposite of this openness, about times when our minds and hearts have been closed and protective. We felt on edge, uneasy, and we usually didn't like ourselves very much. In that kind of a state, we had very few resources to deal with any discomfort or confusion. We were often thrown off balance by even small setbacks. Painful or difficult experiences often overwhelmed us and sent us running for the temporary relief of substances or behaviors.

As we get more comfortable with a generous, open heart, we experience more balance and ease. When something unpleasant arises, we don't have to worry that it's going to crush us or overpower us. We have a refuge we can increasingly rely on in times of trouble. And when a pleasant experience arises, we don't cling to it as desperately, because we don't actually need it to feel good about ourselves.

We also practice generosity to be of service to others, to extend healing and happiness to all beings, and to try in some small way to reduce the suffering in this world.

What we learn as we continue to work with generosity is that the inner practice of recognizing the emptiness of our attachments and building up resilience is one and the same as the outer practice of giving and service.

Recovery is Possible

In the pages of this book is a path, a set of principles and practices, that can lead to the end of our suffering and see us through the damage that we piled onto ourselves through our addictions. The path is based on gaining and maintaining *mindfulness* of our feelings, bodies, minds, and experiences. During our journey, we come to accept that we're responsible for our own actions, and that every choice has a consequence. If we act unskillfully or mindlessly, we will experience pain in our own feelings, thoughts, and experiences (*karma*), and we may cause harm to others. We begin to recognize that every thought, feeling, and experience is only temporary *(impermanence)*, that it will pass if we allow it to, and trusting this can provide a safe harbor in moments of craving or pain. We start to believe that even the most difficult, traumatic, and painful actions and events of our past don't define who we are today, nor do they define the possibilities in our future. It is our choices and actions *now* that define us.

At the same time, we can start to notice and reflect on experience without getting attached to it or to the stories we tell ourselves about it (*selflessness*). We come to accept that we can never satisfy all of our desires and craving. We see this in our struggles with impermanence, with sickness and aging, not getting what we want or or losing what we have, not feeling loved by those we desire or feeling rejected by those whose caring we want the most. We sometimes have to deal with people and situations that are painful or uncomfortable (*unsatisfactoriness*).

But with clear understanding, we can begin to choose more appropriate actions and responses to our experience, and it is in this choice that we find freedom and relief from suffering. When we act with full awareness of each choice, of even the smallest action, we can begin to notice the motivations behind everything we do. We can begin to ask, "Is this action useful or not? Is it skillful or unskillful?" Whenever we're confused or feel lost, we have meditation tools that we can use to simply return to the present moment, to our experience of the present as it is for us *right now,* and we can check in with our sangha—our wise friends—for added perspective and compassionate support.

So, what do we gain by practicing understanding, ethical conduct, and mindfulness? We're asked to sit with discomfort, to experience it without fear or resistance, and to know that it's impermanent. We learn that dukkha is part of the human condition, and efforts to avoid or deny it lead to more unhappiness and suffering. We've learned that we can never satisfy our desires through sense experiences, through chasing pleasure and trying to hold onto it. Every pleasant sense experience will end, and the more we try to hold onto it and turn desire into need or craving, the more we suffer dukkha. We're mindful that dissatisfaction and unhappiness have beginnings. By tracing the dissatisfaction or unhappiness back to its root, we can weed it out of the mind.

We follow the Eightfold Path, which allows us to develop understanding. It teaches us the karmic advantage of compassion, lovingkindness, appreciative joy, and equanimity. We learn the quiet satisfaction of living a more ethical and mindful life.

What we are achieving is what in Buddhism is called **sukha**, or true happiness. This is not the temporary pleasure that comes from a high or other temporary sense experience, but the inner peace and well-being that comes from a balanced, mindful life. It is the opposite of the suffering and unsatisfactoriness of dukkha. Sukha is freedom from hate, greed and confusion. It is an expansive approach to life, being able to sit with and move through feelings of discomfort, dissatisfaction, and discontent. Many of us have been running from and denying dukkha for a very long time, but we have found that it is only when we stop running that we are able to truly access authentic happiness. We can practice the message:

> I am here.
> This is the way it is *right now*.
> This is a moment of suffering. May I give myself the care I need at this moment.
> May I accept this without struggling, but also without giving up.

We've started to learn that mindfulness involves investigating our unskillful actions and choices, both past and present, and choosing to act with more wisdom in the future. Rather than being bogged down by guilt or shame about the past, we can use it as a guide to making different choices in the present. As we devote energy to awakening and recovery, we'll learn to investigate our present and our past with wisdom rather than craving or aversion. We'll experience the growth of trust in our own capacity for, and right to, recovery.

As we get a clearer understanding of what we're doing in our lives, of the choices we are making and the consequences of those choices, we gain the opportunity to develop generosity, lovingkindness, forgiveness, and equanimity. These are central to Buddhist practice, and to our recovery. We learn to give freely, because we understand that clinging to what is "mine" is based on the delusion that we are what we possess, or what we control. We learn to have *metta*, or lovingkindness, toward all beings in the world, whether we know them or not.

We come to understand that our practice isn't just for ourselves, but is based on the interconnectedness and happiness of all living beings. Recovery transforms how we show up for those around us. We can become the compassionate, generous, and wise friend whose calming voice and steadfast support can help others to understand their own struggles and find their own path to healing.

There is no magic bullet, no single action or practice that will end suffering. This is a path composed of a set of practices that help us deal with suffering and respond wisely to our own lives. We cannot escape or avoid dukkha, but we can begin to be more at peace knowing there is a path forward: a path with less suffering, less craving, less aversion, less destruction, and less shame. It's a path without an end. It requires effort and awareness. And we don't have to do it alone.

Recovery is the lifelong process of recovering our true natures and finding a way to an enduring and non-harmful sense of happiness. In recovery, we can finally find the peace so many of us had been searching for in our addictions. We can break through our isolation and find a community of wise friends to support us on our path. We can build a home for ourselves, *within* ourselves, and we can help others do the same. The gift we give to ourselves, to one another, and to the world, is one of courage, understanding, compassion, and serenity. We all experience growth differently, and at our own pace. But the most important message of this book is that the journey, the healing, can start now for you and for each of us.

May you find your path to recovery. May you trust in your own potential for awakening.

APPENDIX

MEDITATIONS

All meditation involves a combination of both mindfulness and concentration–*mindfulness* being the more receptive state of observing the mind and noticing thoughts and sensations; *concentration* being the more active energy of choosing what to focus on, whether it be a gentle returning to the breath or training the mind through repeating phrases or mantras.

The Buddha taught four different ways of meditation: sitting, standing, lying down, or walking. You can use any posture that suits you, but be mindful when you are practicing in a group to try not to move in a way that might distract or disturb others. There are many different practices to explore outside the meeting, including mindfulness meditation, concentration meditation, guided meditation, silent meditation, and moving meditations such as walking, yoga, tai chi, or qi gong.

Meditation can bring up powerful emotions, especially for those in early recovery, with histories of trauma, or with co-occurring mental health issues. Silent sitting meditation may not always be the right practice for everyone, every time. If you find yourself caught up by overwhelming emotions, you can "tap the brakes" during practice in a few ways: by opening the eyes; taking a few deep slow breaths; placing a hand over your heart or belly; focusing attention on a soothing object; or imagining a positive place, activity, or memory. Remember to be kind and gentle with yourself. It's always okay to take care of yourself during meditation.

There are many different traditions of Buddhism with many different styles of meditation. Here, we offer a basic template that you may build on with some of the suggested options. Meditation is a personal practice, and we encourage you to explore with a spirit of openness and curiosity. May you find refuge and wisdom in your practice.

Basic Meditation

You can use the script below to lead yourself or others through a meditation. It begins with awareness of breath, which can be a complete practice on its own. There are also optional extensions you can use to practice with: Awareness of Sound, Awareness of Feeling Tone, Awareness of Body Sensations, or Awareness of Processes of the Mind. Read the meditation until you come to the ✳ symbol; then continue with the meditation you selected.

Sit in a comfortable but attentive posture, allowing your back to be straight but not rigid or stiff. Feel your head balanced on your shoulders, allow you face and jaw to relax, with arms and hands resting in a comfortable position.

Be attentive to what's happening within your own awareness, right here and right now, without judgment.

As you sit, begin to notice the **sensations of breath.**

Pay attention for a moment to how your abdomen moves on each in-breath and out-breath, the movement of air through your nostrils, the slight movement of your chest and shoulders.

Find the spot in your body where the sensation of breathing is most vivid, whether it be your abdomen, your chest or your shoulders, or the movement of air through your nostrils. See how fully aware you can be of your whole cycle of breathing, recognizing that each part of the cycle is different from the other part.

(pause)

You will notice your attention shifting away from the breath from time to time. It's perfectly normal for thoughts to wander into fantasies, memories, worries, or things you need to do. When you notice your mind has wandered, try to meet it with a spirit of friendliness. You don't need to *do* anything about it. There is nothing to *fix*. Rather than forcing it, just try to allow yourself to become curious about what it's like to be breathing right now, and you'll find that the attention is naturally drawn back to the physical sensations of breath as it moves through your body.

Stay alert, relaxed, and above all, compassionate, as you maintain awareness of where the mind goes. Each time you notice the mind has been distracted or has wandered, gently shift your awareness back to sensations of breath. (*pause*)

Notice the tendency to want to control your breathing. Let the quality of attention be light and easy, one of simply observing and noticing. You don't need to control the duration, intensity, pace, or the pause between each breath. Just be present.

(*pause*)

As this meditation comes to an end, recognize that you spent this time intentionally aware of your moment-to-moment experience, building the capacity for opening the senses to the vividness, to the change, to the aliveness of the present moment, expanding your skill to be curious about, and open to, whatever presents itself, without judgment.

Then, whenever you're ready, allow your eyes to open and gently bring your attention back to the space you're in.

Awareness of Sound

✦ You may notice that there are **sounds** that come from inside or outside the space you're in, sounds of traffic, the movement of others in the room, or something else going on. If your attention has been drawn by the sound, just be aware of it. Stay with it long enough to notice the quality of the sound–vibration, tone, volume or intensity–being aware of the urge of the mind to label sound: as traffic, as voices, as music, etc. Try to experience the sound without the labels we put on it. Practice recognizing it as just vibrations in the eardrums, just hearing.

Once you've noticed the sound, let it go and bring your attention back to the breath. Let your breath be your anchor of awareness. Each time your awareness goes somewhere else, you can just gently come back to breath, without judgment.

Awareness of Feeling Tone

✦ Notice the tendency to **have an opinion** about things–liking the way things are going right now, not liking it, or sometimes feeling neutral. This tendency can also be an object of awareness. We can practice just noticing that there is an opinion or feeling about how things are *right now*.

When you notice the sensation of liking or pleasure, you can silently tell yourself, "So, this is my liking mind," or "Hello, attachment." When you notice the sensation of not liking, you may know, "So that's my critical mind," or "Hello, aversion," or "So this is what it feels like to want things to be different than they are." We can learn how to notice our pleasant and unpleasant feelings about thoughts and experiences, without judgment and without having to do anything about it.

As you notice that happening, just bring your awareness back to the physical sensations of breath wherever it's most vivid for you, just riding the entire cycle of breathing, one cycle after another.

Awareness of Body Sensations

❀ You may notice your attention shifting to **body sensations**–coolness or warmth, the pressure of your seat on the chair or cushion, maybe achiness, discomfort, or tension. As you become aware of each sensation, notice precisely where it is in the body. Try to notice it in its fullness, how your experience is in this moment with the actual physical sensations of pressure, throbbing, warmth, pulling, or tingling, without judgment or labels. Just notice that it's possible to stay for a moment longer with that sensation, experienced as pure sensation, without the labels of good or bad, pleasurable or unpleasurable. Can you stay with the experience without having to react to it? Just for this moment, be curious about it: How big is it? Does the sensation have a texture or weight? What quality does it have? How is it changing over time?

If there is a strong feeling of physical discomfort that is making it hard to stay focused on the breath, pause before acting on the impulse to move. Bring full awareness to the feeling, and once you're aware of where that is and understand your intention to change the discomfort, move with full mindfulness of your action.

Awareness of Processes of the Mind

❋ As you meditate, notice **where the mind goes**, in terms of thoughts: liking or disliking; perceptions or sensations; hearing of sound; or feelings of peace, sadness, joy, frustration, or anticipation. Just notice these raw thought forms, and then return awareness to sensations of the movement of breath.

If your mind has gone off on a fantasy, thought, judgment, worry, sensation, or sound, just notice in a friendly way that this is happening and come back to the breath. Recognize that the awareness of the distraction is important to this experience, both the movement away from breath and the coming back.

Notice how one thought leads to another, and then another. In those moments when you get lost in thought or your awareness goes somewhere else, see if it is possible to notice the moment when that flicker of awareness happens, when you recognize that your mind has wandered. *This* is a moment of mindfulness. You can acknowledge yourself for noticing you've gone somewhere else, and then just easily bring your attention back to breath in a friendly and non-judgmental way.

Metta (Lovingkindness) Meditation

Find a comfortable but alert position in which to sit. As you allow your eyes to gently close, pay attention to the body and see if there are any minor adjustments that will help you maintain the position for the duration of the meditation. Rest your hands comfortably on your legs or in your lap.

We'll start with a few minutes of concentration practice, just to help our minds settle and arrive in our present-time experience. Allow your breathing to be natural, seeing where in the body you can feel the breath most naturally. It may be in the stomach or abdomen, where you can feel the rising and falling as the body breathes. It might be in the chest, where you may notice the expansion and contraction as the body inhales and exhales. Perhaps it's at the nostrils, where you can feel a slight tickle as the air comes in, and the subtle warmth as the body exhales.

Breathing in, just bring a gentle awareness to the breath. Breathing out, be aware of the breath leaving the body.

(pause)

You may notice the mind wandering. This offers us an opportunity to cultivate mindfulness and concentration. Each time we notice the mind wandering, we're strengthening our ability to recognize our present experience. Each time we bring the mind back to the breath, we strengthen our ability to concentrate. Treat it as an opportunity rather than a problem.

(pause)

Now begin offering mettā (lovingkindness) to yourself. We start with ourselves because without loving ourselves it is almost impossible to love others.

Breathe gently, and repeat silently to yourself the following phrases, or any other phrases of your choosing that communicate a kind and friendly intention:

"May I be filled with lovingkindness."
"May I be safe from inner and outer dangers."
"May I be well in body, heart, and mind."
"May I be at ease and happy."

Repeat these phrases several times, perhaps picturing yourself receiving them. If that is difficult, it can sometimes be helpful to picture yourself as a child receiving this love. Feelings contrary to lovingkindness, like irritation, anger, or doubt, may come up for you. If this happens, be patient with yourself, allowing whatever arises to be received in a spirit of kindness, and then simply return to the phrases.

(two to three minutes of silence)

Now bring to mind someone who has benefitted you or been especially kind. This may be a loved one, a friend, a teacher, or mentor. As this person comes to mind, tune into your natural desire to see this person happy, free from suffering, and at ease with life. Begin to offer this person the same phrases of lovingkindness and care:

"May you be filled with lovingkindness."
"May you be safe from inner and outer dangers."
"May you be well in body, heart, and mind."
"May you be at ease and happy."

(two to three minutes of silence)

Let this person go, and bring to mind a neutral person. This is someone you see, maybe regularly, but don't know very well. It may be somebody who works somewhere you go a lot, a co-worker, a person you've seen at meetings, or maybe a neighbor.

Although you don't know this person well, you can recognize that just as you wish to be happy, this person wants to be happy as well. You don't need to know what their happiness looks like. Again, offer this person the phrases of lovingkindness:

"May you be filled with lovingkindness."
"May you be safe from inner and outer dangers."
"May you be well in body, heart, and mind."
"May you be at ease and happy."

(two to three minutes of silence)

Now, letting this neutral person go, think of somebody whom you find difficult, or toward whom you feel a resentment, hurt, or jealousy. You may not want to pick the most difficult person in your life; instead, choose someone who is currently agitating or annoying you.

Again, offer the phrases of lovingkindness, being aware that just as you wish to be happy and free from harm, so do even the most difficult or troublesome people:

"May you be filled with lovingkindness."
"May you be safe from inner and outer dangers."
"May you be well in body, heart, and mind."
"May you be at ease and happy."

(two to three minutes of silence)

Letting this difficult person go, try to expand your well wishes as wide as you can imagine–to your family, your friends, your community, your city, your state, your

82

country, to all beings on earth. Notice the immense depth of your own heart as you offer these phrases:

"May all beings be filled with lovingkindness."
"May all beings be safe from inner and outer dangers."
"May all beings be well in body, heart, and mind."
"May all beings be at ease and happy."

(two to three minutes of silence)

Now, letting go of all thoughts of others, return your focus to your own body, mind, and heart. Notice any discomfort, tension, or difficulty you are experiencing. Notice if you are experiencing any new lightness, warmth, relaxation, or joy. Then, whenever you are ready, allow your eyes to open and gently return your attention to the space around you.

Forgiveness Meditation

Find a comfortable but alert position in which to sit. As you allow your eyes to gently close, pay attention to the body and see if there are any minor adjustments that will help you maintain the position for the duration of the meditation. Rest your hands comfortably on your legs or in your lap.

We'll start with a few minutes of concentration practice, just to help our minds settle and arrive in our present-time experience. Allow your breathing to be natural, seeing where in the body you can feel the breath most naturally. It may be in the stomach or abdomen, where you can feel the rising and falling as the body breathes. It might be in the chest, where you may notice the expansion and contraction as the body inhales and exhales. Perhaps it's at the nostrils, where you can feel a slight tickle as the air comes in, and the subtle warmth as the body exhales.

Breathing in, just bring a gentle awareness to the breath. Breathing out, be aware of the breath leaving the body.

(pause)

You may notice the mind wandering. This offers us an opportunity to cultivate mindfulness and concentration. Each time we notice the mind wandering, we're strengthening our ability to recognize our present experience. Each time we bring the mind back to the breath, we strengthen our ability to concentrate. Treat it as an opportunity rather than a problem.

(pause)

84

Now, begin offering forgiveness to yourself. We start with ourselves because it is almost impossible to truly forgive others while we still harbor self-resentment.

There are many ways that we have hurt and harmed ourselves. We have betrayed or abandoned ourselves many times through thoughts, words, or actions, knowingly or unknowingly.

Feel your own precious body and life, as you are today. Let yourself become aware of the ways you have hurt or harmed yourself. Picture them, remember them. Be open to the sorrow you have carried from this and give yourself permission to release these burdens.

Breathing gently, repeat silently to yourself the following phrases:

"I forgive myself for the ways I have hurt myself through action or inaction."
"I know I have acted out of fear, pain, and confusion, and for today, I offer myself forgiveness."
"I forgive myself."

Repeat these phrases, letting the feelings permeate your body and mind. Feelings contrary to forgiveness, like irritation, guilt, and anger, may come up for you. If this happens, be patient and kind toward yourself, allowing whatever arises to be received in a spirit of friendliness and kind affection, and simply return to the phrases.

(three minutes of silence)

There are also many ways that you have been harmed by others. You may have been abused or abandoned, knowingly or unknowingly, in thoughts, words, or actions.

Let yourself picture and remember these hurts. Be open to the sorrow you have carried from these actions of others in the past, and give yourself permission to release this burden of pain—at least for today—by extending forgiveness, when your heart is ready.

Bring to mind the people who have hurt you, and then silently repeat the following phrases:

"I now remember the ways you have hurt or harmed me, out of your own fear, pain, confusion, and anger."
"I have carried this pain in my heart too long. At least for today, I offer you forgiveness."
"To all those who have caused me harm, I offer my forgiveness."
"I forgive you."

(three minutes of silence)

There are also many ways that we have hurt and harmed others, have betrayed or abandoned them, have caused them suffering. We have caused harm, knowingly or unknowingly, out of our own pain, fear, anger, and confusion.

Let yourself remember and visualize the ways you have hurt others. Picture each memory that still burdens your heart. Acknowledge the pain you have caused out of your own fear and confusion. Be open to your own sorrow and regret. Give yourself permission to finally release this burden and ask for forgiveness.

Offer each person in your mind the following phrase:

"I know I have harmed you through my thoughts, words, or actions, and I ask for your forgiveness."

(three minutes of silence)

86

Now, letting go of all thoughts of others, return your focus to your own body, mind, and heart. Notice any discomfort, tension, or difficulty you may be feeling. Notice if you are experiencing any new lightness, warmth, relaxation, relief, or joy. Then, whenever you are ready, allow your eyes to open and gently return your attention to the space around you.

Equanimity Meditation

Find a comfortable but alert position in which to sit. As you allow your eyes to gently close, pay attention to the body and see if there are any minor adjustments that will help you maintain the position for the duration of the meditation. Rest your hands comfortably on your legs or in your lap.

We'll start with a few minutes of concentration practice, just to help our minds settle and arrive in our present-time experience. Allow your breathing to be natural, seeing where in the body you can feel the breath most naturally. It may be in the stomach or abdomen, where you can feel the rising and falling as the body breathes. It might be in the chest, where you may notice the expansion and contraction as the body inhales and exhales. Perhaps it's at the nostrils, where you can feel a slight tickle as the air comes in, and the subtle warmth as the body exhales.

Breathing in, just bring a gentle awareness to the breath. Breathing out, be aware of the breath leaving the body.

(pause)

You may notice the mind wandering. This offers us an opportunity to cultivate mindfulness and concentration. Each time we notice the mind wandering, we're strengthening our ability to recognize our present experience. Each time we bring the mind back to the breath, we strengthen our ability to concentrate. Treat it as an opportunity rather than a problem.

(pause)

In equanimity practice, we're cultivating a mind and heart that stays balanced and at ease with our surroundings. In equanimity, we come to understand that our happiness and suffering are not caused by our experiences and circumstances, but in our responses to them.

We may begin our equanimity practice by repeating the following phrases for ourselves:

"I am responsible for my own actions."
"I am responsible for the energy and attention I give my thoughts, feelings, and experiences."
"May I find a true source of happiness."
"May I find peace exactly where I am."

(two to three minutes of silence)

Now bring to mind someone who has benefitted you or been especially kind to you. This may be a loved one, a friend, a teacher, or mentor. As this person comes to mind, tune into your natural desire to see this person happy, free from suffering, and at ease with life.

The practice is to recognize that although we may offer this person compassion, we are not in control of their happiness. Equanimity helps us to let go of the outcome and focus on our own practice.

Repeat silently to yourself the following phrases:

"Regardless of my wishes for you, your happiness is not in my hands."
"All beings are responsible for the suffering or happiness created by their own actions."
"May you find a true source of happiness."
"May you find peace exactly where you are."

(two to three minutes of silence)

Let this person go from your mind and bring to mind a neutral person. This is someone you see, maybe regularly, but don't know very well. It may be somebody who works somewhere you go a lot, a co-worker, a person you've seen at meetings, or maybe a neighbor.

Although you don't know this person well, you can recognize that just as you wish to be happy, this person wants to be happy as well. You don't need to know what their happiness looks like. Again, offer this person the phrases of equanimity, recognizing that you aren't in charge of their happiness.

"Regardless of my wishes for you, your happiness is not in my hands."
"All beings are responsible for the suffering or happiness created by their own actions."
"May you do what needs to be done to find happiness."
"May you find peace exactly where you are."

(two to three minutes of silence)

Now, letting this neutral person go, think of somebody whom you find difficult, or toward whom you feel resentment, hurt, or jealousy. You may not want to pick the most difficult person in your life; instead, choose someone who is currently agitating or annoying you.

Again, offer these phrases of equanimity with the intention of recognizing that they are in charge of their happiness and ease:

"Regardless of my wishes for you, your happiness is not in my hands."
"All beings are responsible for the suffering or happiness created by their own actions."
"May you find a true source of happiness."
"May you find peace exactly where you are."

(two to three minutes of silence)

90

Now, letting go of all thoughts of others, return your focus to your own body, mind, and heart. Notice any discomfort, tension, or difficulty you may be feeling. Notice if you are experiencing any new lightness, warmth, relaxation, or joy. Notice if you feel any increase in your ability to care without controlling, to accept that each of us is responsible for the consequences of our own actions. Then, whenever you are ready, allow your eyes to open and gently return your attention to the space around you.

QUESTIONS FOR INQUIRY

These Questions for Inquiry are intended to be a useful tool for supporting our growth and recovery. They can be used as part of a formal process of self-investigation or inventory with a mentor, wise friend, or group; as tools to explore a specific life situation; as guides for a daily self-inquiry practice; as meeting discussion topics; or any other way you may find helpful on your path of awakening and freedom from addiction and habitual behavior.

Questions for Inquiry of the First Noble Truth:

Begin by making a list of the behaviors and actions associated with your addiction(s) that you consider harmful. Without exaggerating or minimizing, think about the things you have done that have caused harm to yourself and others.

For each behavior listed, write how you have suffered because of that behavior, and write how others have suffered because of that behavior. List any other costs or negative consequences you can think of, such as finances, health, relationships, sexual relations, or missed opportunities.

Do you notice any patterns? What are they? What are the ways that you might avoid or reduce suffering for yourself and others if you change these patterns?

How have your addictive behaviors been a response to trauma and pain? What are some ways you can respond to trauma and pain that nurture healing rather than avoiding?

Questions for Inquiry of the Second Noble Truth:

List situations, circumstances, and feelings that you may have used harmful behavior to try and avoid.

List the emotions, sensations, and thoughts that come to mind when you abstain. Are there troubling memories, shame, grief, or unmet needs hiding behind the craving? How can you meet these with compassion and patience?

What things did you give up in your desire to cling to impermanent and unreliable solutions? For example: did you give up relationships, financial security, health, opportunities, legal standing, or other important things to maintain your addictive behaviors? What made the addiction more important to you than any of these things you gave up?

Are there any beliefs you cling to that fuel craving and aversion, beliefs that deny the truth of impermanence, or beliefs about how things in life "should" be? What are they?

Questions for Inquiry of the Third Noble Truth:

What makes it so hard to quit?

What resources are available to help you abstain and recover?

List reasons to believe you can recover. Also list your doubts. What might the wise and compassionate part of you—your Buddha nature—say about these doubts?

Practice "letting go" of something small. Notice that the craving doesn't last and that there's a little sense of relief when you let it pass. That's a little taste of freedom.

Questions for Inquiry of the Fourth Noble Truth:

Understanding that recovery and the ending of suffering is possible, what is your path to recovery and ending the suffering of addiction? Be honest about the challenges you might face, and the tools and resources you will use to meet those challenges.

What behavior can you change to more fully support your recovery?

What does it mean to you to take refuge in the Buddha, the Dharma, and the Sangha for your recovery?

Questions for Inquiry of Wise Understanding:

Think of a situation in your life that is causing confusion or unease.

- What is the truth of this situation?
- Are you seeing clearly, or are you getting lost in judgment, taking things personally, in stories you're telling yourself, or repeating past messages you've internalized? How?

- Is your vision clouded by greed, hatred, confusion, clinging, attachment, or craving? How?

In what situations and parts of your life do you have the most difficulty separating desire from need? Are there areas or relationships where the drive to get what you desire overshadows any other consideration? Has this changed as you began or continue in recovery?

Are there parts of your life where you are driven to continue unpleasant experiences because you think you "must" or "need to?"

How is karma—the law of cause and effect—showing up right now? Where in your life are you dealing with the effects or aftermath of action you took in the past, both positive and negative?

Questions for Inquiry of Wise Intention:

During your periods of addictive behavior, how did you act in ways that were clinging, uncaring, harsh, cruel, or unforgiving? Toward whom (including yourself) were these feelings directed? How might generosity, compassion, lovingkindness, and forgiveness have changed your behavior?

What actions have you taken that have harmed others?

Have you formed an intention to reconcile with both yourself and the person or people you've harmed (to make amends)? If so, have you found a wise friend or mentor you can go to for guidance and support in the amends process, which is summarized below? What support can this person provide as you begin the process of amends?

Making Amends:

- Have you done something intentionally that you now recognize caused harm to another? Who has been harmed by your actions?
- Have you honestly formed the intention not to repeat harmful actions and to learn from the experience in future interactions? Have you begun the process of directly addressing the harmful actions of your past?
- Making amends depends on the circumstance, including your present relationship to the person and the extent to which you can undo the harm caused through direct actions (like correcting a public dishonesty or compensating another for things you have taken that were not freely offered). Ask yourself, "What can I do in the present?"
- Can you address and reconcile with the harm you have caused without forming an attachment to being forgiven? Identify the motivation for making each amends.
- What actions would restore balance in your own feelings and approach to whatever harm you have caused? Can these steps be taken without causing new harm to the person or the relationship?

If you're experiencing a difficult situation or choice in your life right now, investigate the intention you are bringing to this situation.

- Are you being selfish or self-seeking? How?
- Are you being driven by aversion (running away from an unpleasant experience) or craving (grasping for pleasure)? How?
- How could you bring in a spirit of generosity, compassion, lovingkindness, appreciative joy, and forgiveness to this situation?
- How would this situation look different if you brought these factors to mind *before* reacting or responding?
- If you don't want to, can you at least have the intention and willingness to do so?

Questions for Inquiry of Wise Speech:

Have you caused harm with your speech? How?

Have you been dishonest or harsh in your communication? When, and in what specific ways?

Do you use speech now to hurt or control people, to present a false idea or image of yourself or of reality, to demand attention, or to relieve the discomfort of silence? Detail specific instances in which you used speech to mislead, misdirect, or distract.

Are you careful to avoid causing harm with your speech?

Do you say things you know are not true, or pretend to know the truth about something when you don't, to appear more knowledgeable or credible than you are? List some examples.

Questions for Inquiry of Wise Action:

Have you acted in a way that was unskillful or that created suffering? How?

During those times you were unskillful or created suffering, how would it have changed the outcome if you had acted out of compassion, kindness, generosity, and forgiveness? Would you now have a different emotional or mental response to your past actions if you had acted with these principles in mind?

First Precept:
- Have you caused harm? How? (Allow for a broad understanding of harm, including physical, emotional, mental, and karmic harm as well as financial, legal, moral, or other forms of harm.)
- Even if you can't point to specific harms that you have caused, have you acted in a way that purposely avoided being aware of the possibility of harm?

Second Precept:
- People "take" in many ways–we take goods or material possessions, we take time and energy, we take care and recognition. With this broad understanding of taking, have you taken what has not been freely given? How? What are specific examples or patterns where this has been true for you?

Third Precept:
- Have you behaved irresponsibly, selfishly, or without full consent and

awareness (from yourself or partners) in your sexual conduct? How?

- Reviewing your sexual partners or activities, have you been fully aware in each instance of other existing relationships, prior or current mental or emotional conditions of yourself and your partner(s), and your own intentions in becoming sexually involved? How or how not?
- Has your sexual activity, both by yourself and with others, been based on non-harmful intentions? Have you entered into each sexual activity with awareness and understanding? How or how not?

Fourth Precept:
- Have you been dishonest? How?
- What patterns did your dishonesty take? Did you act or speak dishonestly to deny or misrepresent the truth about your own behavior or status?
- Were there particular situations in which your dishonesty was particularly present (for instance: when dealing with your addictive behaviors, in job or professional settings, among friends, with family)? Investigate the source of the dishonesty in each setting–was it based on greed, confusion, fear, denial? Why were you lying?

Fifth Precept:

- Have you used intoxicants or other behaviors that cloud your ability to see clearly?
- What substances and behaviors have you become reliant on to change or cloud your awareness? Has this changed over time, or, if you have periods of abstinence, were your habitual intoxicants or behaviors replaced by other ways to avoid awareness of your present circumstances and conditions? How?

Questions for Inquiry of Wise Livelihood:

Does your job cause harm? What is the specific nature of that harm?

How can you do your job more mindfully and with an intention of compassion and non-harm?

Do you bring an understanding of karma and kindness to your job, or do you compartmentalize it and exclude it from awareness of wise action?

What part does greed play in the choices you make in your livelihood? Does greed get in the way of awareness or compassion?

How can you be of more service in your community?

How might you bring a spirit of generosity to your life, both in your profession and outside it?

Questions for Inquiry of Wise Effort:

What efforts have you made to connect with a wise friend, mentor, or dharma buddy who can help you develop and balance your efforts?

Think of a situation that is causing you discomfort or unease. What is the nature of the effort you're bringing to the situation? Pay attention to whether it feels balanced and sustainable, or if you're leaning too far in the direction of either inactivity or overexertion?

Are you dealing with overwhelming desires, aversions, laziness or discouragement, restlessness and worry, or doubt about your own ability to recover? How do these hindrances affect the choices you're making?

Are you avoiding feelings by checking out and giving up, or through obsessive busyness and perfectionism?

Questions for Inquiry of Wise Mindfulness:

What are steps you can take to support a regular meditation practice?

What are steps you can take to practice mindfulness more throughout the day by checking in with yourself about how you're feeling, and pausing before reacting to situations?

What are steps you can take to sit with your discomfort instead of running from it or running toward temporary pleasure?

What are steps you can take to question the "truths" that your mind tells you, rather than automatically believing them? Identify specific instances where your mind and perceptions "lied" to you about the truth of a situation, and how being aware of that might have changed your reaction and led to a less harmful outcome.

Think about times when you felt fear, doubt, or hesitation. Now bring an awareness of their temporary nature. How might that awareness have led to an outcome that was less harmful?

Questions for Inquiry of Wise Concentration:

How do you get unfocused or distracted in meditation? What distracts you the most?
What are steps you can take to refocus your mind without judging your own practice?
Notice what value or learning you could gain by carefully and kindly noticing where your mind has gone, or what has distracted you.

What are steps you can take to use concentration to see clearly and act wisely?

What are steps you can take to be kind and gentle with yourself through this process?

)SSARY

the followers of the Buddha
ʒs when he died in the fifth
·rve them, the teachings were
ɔo generation after generation of
ɣ were finally written down,
i language.

ɘ still described in Pāli, or in a
ɡuage called Sanskrit, because
late into English. Therefore, the
are only rough approximations,
to deepen the understanding of
words through reflection and

Budᴀ... ...... ᴄrit): a personal title, meaning
"the awakened one ᴏᴦ "the enlightened one;" most
commonly used for Siddhārtha Gautama Buddha, the
founder of Buddhism.

Dāna (Pāli and Sanskrit): Generosity; charity.
Traditionally refers to the giving of alms or donations to
monastic or spiritually-developed people.

Dharma (Sanskrit; **Dhamma** in Pāli): the teachings of
the **Buddha**; the nature of reality; phenomena.

Dukkha (Pāli; **Duḥkha** in Sanskrit): sorrow; stress;
unsatisfactoriness; the suffering in life caused by
clinging to temporary phenomena as if they were
permanent.

Kalyāṇa-mitta (Pāli; **Kalyāṇa-mitra** in Sanskrit): good
friend; wise companion; a teacher or mentor in
understanding the **Dharma**.

Karma (Sanskrit; **Kamma** in Pāli): action; doing; cause and effect; intentional activity that leads to immediate and future consequence(s).

Karuṇā (Pāli and Sanskrit): compassion; kindness; the desire for harm and suffering to be removed from oneself and others.

Mettā (Pāli; **Maitrī** in Sanskrit): lovingkindness; benevolence; friendliness; goodwill; an active desire for the well-being and happiness of oneself and others.

Muditā (Pāli and Sanskrit): the sympathetic, appreciative joy in the success and happiness of others.

Saṅgha (Pāli; **Saṃgha** in Sanskrit): traditionally, the communities of Buddhist monks and nuns; followers of the **Buddha**, whether monastics or lay-people.

Sukha (Pāli and Sanskrit): quiet joy; ease; unhindered flow; the opposite of **Dukkha**.

Upekkhā (Pāli; **Upekṣā** in Sanskrit): equanimity; evenness of mind; serenity; unshakeable freedom of mind; a state of inner equipoise that cannot be upset by gain and loss.

RECOVERY DHARMA
MEETING FORMAT

This script is meant to serve as a suggested template. Individual meetings may choose to edit it or use other formats to meet the needs of their sangha.

Before the meeting, the facilitator may find volunteers to read the following:
- *The Practice*
- *The Four Noble Truths and Eightfold Path*
- *The Dedication of Merit*

OPENING

Welcome to this meeting of _____. We are gathered to explore a Buddhist-inspired approach to recovery from addiction of all kinds. We are peer-led and do not follow any one leader or teacher, but trust in the wisdom of the Buddha (the potential for our own awakening), the Dharma (the truth, or the teachings), and the Sangha (our community of wise friends on this path). This is a program of empowerment and doesn't ask us to believe in anything other than our own potential to change and heal. We have found a guide for our recovery in the Buddhist teachings of the Four Noble Truths and the Eightfold Path, and we invite you to investigate these practices and principles as tools for your own path of liberation from the suffering of addiction. We understand that this is not the only path to recovery and many may choose to combine these practices with other recovery programs.

My name is _____ and I am the facilitator of this

meeting. I am not a Buddhist teacher, nor do I have any particular authority in this meeting. I am a member of this community and have volunteered to help lead our meeting and discussion today.

I have asked _____ to read **The Practice**:

THE PRACTICE

Renunciation: We understand *addiction* to describe the overwhelming craving and compulsive use of substances or behaviors in order to escape present-time reality, either by clinging to pleasure or running from pain. We commit to the intention of abstinence from alcohol and other addictive substances. For those of us recovering from process addictions, particularly those for which complete abstinence is not possible, we also identify and commit to wise boundaries around our harmful behaviors, preferably with the help of a mentor or therapeutic professional.

Meditation: We commit to the intention of developing a daily meditation practice. We use meditation as a tool to investigate our actions, intentions, and reactivity. Meditation is a personal practice, and we commit to finding a balanced effort toward this and other healthy practices that are appropriate to our own journey on the path.

Meetings: We attend recovery meetings whenever possible, in person and/or online. Some may wish to be part of other recovery fellowships and Buddhist communities. In early recovery, it is recommended to attend a recovery meeting as often as possible. For many that may mean every day. We also commit to becoming an active part of the community, offering our own experiences and service wherever possible.

The Path: We commit to deepening our understanding of the Four Noble Truths and to practicing the Eightfold Path in our daily lives.

Inquiry and Investigation: We explore the Four Noble Truths as they relate to our addictive behavior through writing and sharing in-depth, detailed Inquiries. These can be worked with the guidance of a mentor, in partnership with a trusted friend, or with a group. As we complete our written Inquiries, we undertake to hold ourselves accountable and take direct responsibility for our actions, which includes making amends for the harm we have caused in our past.

Sangha, Wise Friends, Mentors: We cultivate relationships within a recovery community, to both support our own recovery and support the recovery of others. After we have completed significant work on our Inquiries, established a meditation practice, and achieved renunciation from our addictive behaviors, we can then become mentors to help others on their path to liberation from addiction. Anyone with any period of time of renunciation and practice can be of service to others in their sangha. When mentors are not available, a group of wise friends can act as partners in self-inquiry and support each other's practice.

Growth: We continue our study of these Buddhist practices through reading, listening to dharma talks, visiting and becoming members of recovery and spiritual sanghas, and attending meditation or dharma retreats when we believe these practices will contribute to our understanding and wisdom. We undertake a lifelong journey of growth and awakening.

I have asked _____ to read the **Four Noble Truths and Eightfold Path**:

THE FOUR NOBLE TRUTHS AND EIGHTFOLD PATH

As people who have struggled with addiction, we are already intimately familiar with the truth of suffering. Even if we have never heard of the Buddha, at some level we already know the foundation of his teachings, which we call the Dharma: that in this life, there is suffering.

The Buddha also taught the way to free ourselves from this suffering. The heart of these teachings is the Four Noble Truths and the corresponding commitments, which are the foundation of our program.

1. There is suffering.
    We commit to understanding the truth of suffering.
2. There is a cause of suffering.
    We commit to understanding that craving leads to suffering.
3. There is an end to suffering.
    We commit to understanding and experiencing that less craving leads to less suffering.
4. There is a path to the end of suffering.
    We commit to cultivating the path.

The Buddha taught that by living ethically,

practicing meditation, and developing wisdom and compassion, we can end the suffering that is created by resisting, running from, and misunderstanding reality. We have found that these practices and principles can end the suffering of addiction. The Eightfold Path helps us find our way in recovery and consists of the following:

1. Wise Understanding
2. Wise Intention
3. Wise Speech
4. Wise Action
5. Wise Livelihood
6. Wise Effort
7. Wise Mindfulness
8. Wise Concentration

INTRODUCTIONS

In an effort to build community and to get to know each other, we start each meeting by introducing ourselves. There is no need to identify yourself by anything other than your name, and if you choose you can also let us know your gender pronoun. My name is _____ (and I use the pronoun ___).

MEDITATION

We will now do a guided meditation on _____. Your eyes may be closed or gently open. Meditation is a personal practice, and we encourage you to explore with a spirit of openness and curiosity. Part of what we are doing is learning to sit with discomfort, but meditation can bring up powerful emotions for some of us, and if you find that you need to "tap the brakes" during practice, you can do so in the following ways: by opening the eyes; taking a few deep slow breaths; placing a hand over your heart or belly; focusing attention on a soothing object; imagining a positive place, activity, or memory; or quietly shifting your position. Remember to be kind and gentle with yourself. It's always okay to take care of yourself during meditation. If you need to get up during the meditation, please do so as quietly as possible, and please hold your comments and questions until after meditation.

(Meetings may be either a Literature Discussion, Topic Discussion, or other format.)

LITERATURE DISCUSSION MEETING

We will now take turns reading from the book *The Dharma of Recovery* (or another Buddhist book), and then open the meeting for discussion.

TOPIC/SPEAKER DISCUSSION MEETING

_____ *(speaker)* will now speak about _____ *(a topic related to recovery and Buddhism, or their experience in addiction and recovery)*, and then we will open the meeting for discussion.

GROUP SHARING

(Meetings choose whether to do tag-pass, facilitator selected, or "popcorn" style sharing.)

Please limit your share to 3 to 5 minutes to ensure that everyone who wants to has a chance to speak. We commit to making this space as safe and welcoming as possible for all members of our community. Please be wise in your speech by trying to use "I" statements and focusing your share on your own experience of addiction, recovery, Buddhist principles and practices, or tonight's topic. We ask that you avoid commenting on another person's share or offering opinions or advice.

CLOSING

That is all the time we have for sharing. Thank you for being with us tonight. In order to respect each others' privacy and to create a safe environment for all who attend, please keep everything that was said in this meeting and who was here confidential. We encourage you to continue your meditation practice, your study of Buddhist principles, and to reach out to others in order to build community. Would anyone who is willing to talk with newcomers after the meeting please raise their hand?

ANNOUNCEMENTS

We now pass the basket for *dāna*, which is a Buddhist term for the practice of generosity. Please give what you can to support the meeting.

(Announcements about clean up, phone/email list, books for sale, free handouts, upcoming retreats, or other news pertaining to the group.)

DEDICATION OF MERIT

We will now close with the dedication of merit:

(Volunteer may read, or pass out copies to read as a group. Individual meetings and sanghas may choose to write their own dedications of merit.)

> Refuge does not arise in a particular place, but in the space within the goodness of our hearts. When this space is imbued with wisdom, respect, and love, we call it sangha. We hope that the pain of addiction, trauma, and feeling "apart" actually leads us back toward the heart and that we might understand compassion, wisdom, and change ever more deeply. As we have learned from practice, great pain does not erase goodness, but in fact informs it.
>
> May we make the best use of our practice, and whatever freedom arises from our efforts here today. May this be a cause and condition for less suffering and more safety in our world.

Made in the USA
Middletown, DE
20 January 2021